BOTTOMS UP!

BOTTOMS UP!

Cornelia Otis Skinner

DRAWINGS BY

alajálov.

Dodd, Mead & Company   NEW YORK

Published March, 1955
Second printing March, 1955

The stories, "The Bard and My Father," "Crying in the
Dark" and "Those Starring Days," appeared originally in
The New Yorker

Library of Congress Catalog Card Number: 55-6932

Printed in the United States of America
by Vail-Ballou Press, Inc., Binghamton, N. Y.

Contents

TO

Walshie

WITH MY LOVE

The Bard and
My Father

The Bard and
My Father

D ANIEL FROHMAN, or "Uncle Dan" as he
was better known by everyone in the theatrical profession, was a sweet, pontifical darling who had a
grandly persuasive way of getting actors to do whatever he wanted, and what he usually wanted was to
have them take part in one of the many benefits he
ran for his pet charity, the Actors' Fund of America.
Actors always acquiesced, partly because of affection
for Uncle Dan, partly because of a superstitious reluctance to deny support to that organization whose
benevolence they might one day need. During the
latter 1920's, Uncle Dan got the notion of staging a
big matinée benefit in Philadelphia. His plan was that

the program would be made up of whatever could be culled in the way of thespian talent from the three or four companies appearing in town, augmented by a few specialty acts imported from New York. As my father who was touring in Sidney Howard's *Sancho Panza* was booked for that week in Philadelphia, Mr. Frohman asked him if he'd take part in the benefit by doing a scene from some play. Father said he'd be delighted and what scene from what play did they have in mind. Uncle Dan said he didn't care but thought a bit of Shakespeare with a suitable leading lady would be quite nice, and leaving the choice up to my father, gave his benediction and departed.

The Shakespearean bit my father chose was the second scene of *Richard III* and the suitable leading lady was myself. How suitable I was at that time, to anyone but a fond parent, is a matter of speculation. I was making gawkishly youthful attempts to be a lady, about which there was little that might have been called leading. As an actress, I was barely fledged, having had a scant two years' professional experience during which I had disappeared in a number of nondescript plays which usually opened in Stamford, played Hartford and Springfield and, if they lasted long enough to open on Broadway, instantly went through the metamorphosis of turning into what *Variety* calls a "turkey." The parts in which I was cast were listed in theatrical agency files under the heading of "Park Avenue type." In the guise of a supposedly aristocratic and slightly acid character, clad in clothes as chic as the management could afford, I'd come on briefly at the beginning of first acts, utter a few expositionary remarks to a butler or another "Park Avenue type" and make my final exit before a good portion of the audience were even seated. The week prior to the proposed Actor's Fund benefit found me playing one *Sally Van Twiller* who, according to the program, was "Robert's sister, a wealthy socialite," in a highly uncomic little comedy which, fortunately for everybody concerned, was breathing its last gags in Pittsburgh.

On Tuesday morning I received a phone call from Father who, that week, was playing Indianapolis. For Father to speak over the long distance wire was as unprecedented a thing for him to do as it was for the person on the other end to hear. Father who loathed and mistrusted all forms of telephonic communication could never get over the feeling that if he were talking to anyone further than ten miles away, he must help out the connection by putting his mouth against the instrument and bellowing. It was worse when he was excited and, as the prospect of any new venture filled him with zestful enthusiasm, the effect in my ear was a blurred blast. Decoding it as best I could, I gathered that I was to go out right away to the nearest bookstore, purchase a copy of *Richard III*, study up on the part of Lady Anne in her opening scene and be ready to go on with him Monday afternoon in Philadelphia. Being a slow reacter to the sudden, it took me some time to get the prospect straight. As his and my schedules were such that we couldn't get together before

Monday morning, I posed the rehearsing problem, which he quickly solved by saying we'd have a few run-throughs up in his hotel room before the show. I then asked what about costumes. This too offered no difficulties to Father who assured me his old *Richard* one must surely be still in good shape (it was some thirty years since he'd last worn it) and as for me, he'd written to Mother back home in New York, to look through the stage trunks and she and I could whip up something over Sunday. I could bring both costumes over with me Monday morning. And he hung up.

I purchased a Temple edition of *Richard III* and, according to Father's instructions which came next day by mail, cut the specified scenes. He had made an arrangement of the first two welded together . . . the famous "winter of our discontent" soliloquy to be followed without interruption by the dramatic episode in which the wily hunchback waylays the widowed Lady Anne on her way to bury her father-in-law King Henry VI, whom he has assassinated and boldly pays court to her before the poor man is so much as deposited in the earth. Needless to say, Father's cuts were for the most part in my speeches, but the part was still effective. I memorized it and, being excessively young, thought myself quite terrific. I thought myself even more terrific when at home on Sunday, Mother and I whipped up that costume. It was less whipped than pinned, but Mother had a great sense of color and period and she managed to create a charmingly authentic effect, complete with Lady-in-a-tower kirtle, peaked headdress with veil, wimple and further Plantagenet accessories. Viewing me with satisfaction Mother said that I looked like an old Abbey. I was reassured to learn that she referred to the romantic painter, not an ecclesiastical structure. She had ferreted from the stage trunks Father's *Richard* attire, with even its original hump, which was beginning to lose some of its sawdust. It reeked of ancient mothballs but Mother doubted if the smell would get across the footlights.

Monday morning I went to Philadelphia, met Father at his hotel and we rehearsed the scene to our own satisfaction and what must have been the considerable astonishment of the occupants of the adjoining rooms. We were both letter perfect in our lines and, as no one else was present to gainsay it, we admitted with simple candor that we were pretty damn good. After the third or fourth run-through, I asked Father what arrangements he had made about the funeral cortège.

"What funeral cortège?" he asked.

"The coffin-bearers," I said. "The ones who carry on King Henry, my dead father-in-law. We can hardly use stage hands."

Father said "oh"; then picking up the telephone he added "I'll call my company manager and tell him to get hold of four men from our cast."

"What about my dead father-in-law?"

"You can always get one over at the theatre."

"Dead fathers-in-law?"

"Oh, a stretcher or some such thing. We'll fake it."

13

And he turned his attention to instructing his manager to commandeer four actors and have them on stage at the Garrick Theatre at 2:30. When I hissed at him, "What about their costumes?" he shouted through the phone ". . . and tell them to have on their clothes from the show."

"Father darling!" I remonstrated, "they'll be the wrong period! Our scene takes place at the end of the War of the Roses in England!" I had just figured this out and was pretty pedantic about it. "Your show is the Cervantes period in Spain . . . some two hundred years later! Your Don Quixote boys will look ridiculous!"

"We'll get them to take their ruffs off. No one'll know the difference." And he added the actor's inevitable "We'll fake it."

Once again we ran through our lines and action, downed some eggs and coffee and at two o'clock drove to the Garrick and ventured through the stage door. Only those who have taken part in benefit shows have any inkling of the acrimonious frenzy and genial pandemonium which reigns backstage during these occasions of benevolent intentions. Actors who arrive and can't find out when they're to go on. Actors who go on and won't come off. Actors who don't ever arrive. Opera singers who have to have hot tea. Specialty artists whose equipment gets locked in a dressing-room to which the key has disappeared and nobody knows who had it last. Pallid committee gentlemen waiting unhappily in the wings clutching financial reports and written speeches which they never get a chance to read. Dance teams fussing about the color of the follow light. Animal acts whose entrance necessitates opening wide the scenery doors and letting in blasts of pneumonia. Electricians and property men hating the whole damned affair. And in the midst of it all, one lone volunteer stage manager trying to run things and rapidly losing his mind.

As we made our way into the traditional turmoil, a young man who seemed to be some sort of assistant to an assistant ran up to Father and exclaimed, "Oh, it's Mr. Skinner. Just a minute and I'll find out where you're to go." Father took a stand by the door and assumed the attitude of patient detachment with which I'd so often seen him confront all aspects of violence, from California earthquakes to French customs porters, and waited. In a few seconds, another assistant ran up to say oh it was Mr. Skinner and just a minute and he'd find out where we were to go. Father continued to wait in his other world and after a few more seconds a third young man ran up and informed Father of his own identity, said we'd not be going on for at least an hour and led us off to our dressing-rooms. Father, being a big star, was allotted one to himself. I, not being even an asteroid, shared the girls' chorus room with sundry performers. There was a pair of wide-eyed twins who had a boop-boop-a-doop act and an actress from an Irish art theatre who was to do a sketch by Synge or Lady Gregory which proved to be very droll, very Gaelic and very impossible to understand.

There was also a lady whose function in show business was to stand in the background with a whip and a dazzling smile while a gentleman made a horse do a lot of things that humans can do much better. They were all agreeably cordial, cleared space for my things on the make-up shelf and the horse lady helped me into my 15th century ensemble which, she said as she eyed her own pink spangles, was "certainly different."

I emerged from the dressing-room and made my way into the wings. Father, striking in costume and make-up, was already there. So were the four Don Quixote boys who had been conscripted as pall-bearers. And they were striking too. Tall, melancholy Spanish grandees, they had been shorn of their ruffs, without which their necks looked curiously long, bare and buzzard-like. They seemed almost indecent. One felt that each should quickly cover up the blatant exposure with something . . . possibly an ice-collar. Even a kidney-basin would not have looked more peculiar. Father himself must have had a few misgivings about them, for he eyed them dubiously for a time, then with rather forced optimism said "Never mind, we'll fake it. The audience shouldn't be watching them any-way," and he turned his attention to the funeral litter which someone had contrived out of an army cot and a velvet piano cover, under which reposed my deceased father-in-law in the form of some dusty pillows. When later the pall-bearers lifted it, they nearly tossed it into the aisles.

Out on the stage a blond, curly baritone was con-

cluding his final hair-on-the-chest selection in which
he was lustily assuring the audience that he was one
of the men who were stouthearted men. The volunteer
impressario in charge of the show informed us our
act would follow immediately, and what did Mr.
Skinner wish for a backdrop. Father allowed as how
plain velvet curtains would be suitable for Shakespeare. The house-manager who was backstage as one
of the many persons getting in other persons' way,
came forward with the information that they had
something even more suitable in the form of a painted
drop representing "an antique English street" which,
he assured us, "for Shakespeare is the ticket" and without waiting for an o.k. he ordered a stage hand to
lower No. 3. The baritone came off, the m.c. announced
our turn, and a special spot blazed on as No. 3 was
impressively lowered. It was easy to see why the
manager considered No. 3 the ticket for Shakespeare,
for it was a painted view of a post-card English village,
complete with beam-and-plaster houses and a thatched
cottage, Ann Hathaway-type. That ticket might have
come in especially handy for the Bard as, at the distant
cross-road, large, red and unmistakable, was a London
bus. This pretty anachronism neither of us noticed until Father was actually starting onto the stage. Father,
at the sight, staggered for a split second and evoked
the Deity, but it was too late to do anything about it.
He hissed at someone to dim the borders and at me
not to mind, we'd fake it, then, nothing daunted, made
his magnificent entrance as the limping villain, to the

thunderous greeting of an adoring public who, in their pleasure at seeing him, would not have cared if the backdrop had represented Main Street and the corner dry-goods store.

The applause was followed by a breathless silence as *Richard's* opening soliloquy rang out in my father's glorious voice. He gave it a perfect reading, finished with fine flourish and, after an effective pause, spoke the cue for the rest of us to come on. The pall-bearers, toting the pillow corpse, were to go on ahead and I was to follow in an appropriate attitude of woe. The bare-necked hidalgos briskly lifted their fragile charge and never was the line about those "pale ashes of the House of Lancaster" more applicable. However, they steadied the flimsy arrangement and, being good actors, were able to carry it on with a certain semblance of realism and, when I came on and told them to "set down their honorable load" they managed to do so without letting it bounce. I spoke Anne's opening speech of sorrowing bereavement and Father came forward with Richard's words of insolent accost to which I responded with the second speech of injured outrage. And at that point something happened to Father.

What brought it about I shall never know. Possibly it was an access of nervousness for me, possibly a blend of emotions at the sudden realization that here, for the first time, he found himself interpreting his favorite playwright with his child who, being an only one, was perforce also his favorite. Whatever the cause, the result was that when I gave him his next cue, he fixed me with a look of utter blankness and said not a word. He simply stood there staring at me as frozen as a contestant in a game of still-pond-no-more-moving, while I, in similar paralysis, stood staring back at him. Finally he broke his living statue pose and came to . . . somewhat. Not to the point yet of speaking but to the extent of resorting to the old stock company trick in which an actor who has suddenly "dried up" tosses the buck to someone else by making it look as though it were his fellow player who had drawn the blank. Assuming a superciliously patient air he eyed me as much as to say "Come, come, my good girl, why can't you speak up?" I continued to stare back at him, as lost as a nocturnal animal dazzled by the nature photographer's flash-bulb. It became hideously clear that my parent had no intention of breaking the silence which was beginning to have a hypnotic effect on the audience. Even the overheated dowager in the front row had stopped beating her bosom with the program and was holding her breath for something to happen. I knew it was up to me to say something so what I said was "O wonderful when devils tell the truth!" which being a direct reply to the lines Father had failed to say must have sounded a bit peculiar.

At this, my father suddenly snapped out of his silence and began to speak and what *he* said was even more peculiar. His state of mind changed from one of blankness to one of furious activity, and one in which every line of *Richard III* fled from it and every line of every Shakespearean play he knew, rushed into it. There were bits of *Hamlet*, snatches of *The Merchant*, oddments from *As You Like It* and an occasional sprinkling of *Much Ado*. Now and then there was some original improvising which Father effected in the most perfect iambic pentameter. It made less than no sense and it all sounded extraordinarily effective for he gave it the assured delivery of the seasoned actor and never by a waver of hesitancy revealed his inner state of whirling confusion. Altogether, it was a triumph as the epitome of "faking it." Every so often he'd pause and when he did, I interpolated my speeches, which, brief as they were, proved to be the only correct ones of the scene to be heard that afternoon. And they too were effective. I spoke them with considerably more hysterical verve than my callow years as an actress would otherwise have permitted, for I was convinced that my father had suddenly gone daft and it was only a strong sense of having to uphold the family name that kept me from going along with him. Toward the end, he did remember to present me with the ring, although to judge by his accompanying words, it might have been the brass one from a Coney Island merry-go-round. Then I had my final say and exited with shaking knees. The moment I'd departed, Father apparently recovered his sanity, for the opening line of his final soliloquy came forth with full emphasis and meaning . . . that line being "Was ever woman in this humor woo'd?" The ensuing words he spoke completely correctly, wrapped his cloak about him with a fine swoop and came off to where I was cowering in the wings. For a second or two we waited for either derisive cat-calls or contemptuous silence. And then, to our incredulous ears there came a roar of applause, the sort that could, in all modesty, have been called a regular ovation. In a state of bewilderment we went on for a number of ill-deserved curtain calls. Father took several alone, then came back to the wings where we stood looking sheepish and feeling like a couple of urchins who have accidentally hurled a brick through a window and have yet to be discovered.

"That was sort of awful" whispered Father.

I could only agree with a whispered uh-huh but added by way of consolation that at least the audience didn't seem to know the difference. "No," he said, "but you can bet your boots Dan Frohman did." Hardly had he voiced this gloomy opinion than Uncle Dan hove into sight. To our astonishment his hand was outstretched and his face was a glow of genial pleasure.

"Congratulations, Otis!" he said, and what's more, he appeared to mean it. "That was the most unique performance of *Richard* I've seen in years!"

Father bleated that indeed it must have been, but didn't enlarge upon the theme. And after a few more utterances of misguided praise from Uncle Dan, we slunk off to our dressing-rooms.

The moral of this tale, I guess, is that people who attend benefit performances just don't listen to Shakespeare. Maybe they don't at any performance.

Where to Look

Where to Look

MAYBE it's a sign of neurosis (and if it is, I hope nobody lets me know) but I am becoming more and more acutely sensitive about those moments when one doesn't know where to look. I first came aware of the problem two or three years ago while lunching with a gentleman in a quiet restaurant where lights were subdued and a quartette played soothing airs amid potted specimens of tropical vegetation. The problem was not concerned in any way with the gentleman. He was a TV agent whom I barely knew, but he was in the throes of an "idea" and lunch was a perfunctory setting for presenting it. The where-to-look difficulty arose from the quartette which, from time to time, ceased to be a quartette and became a trio as the first violinist stepped down off the platform to stroll about the room, still playing and pausing soulfully before various tables for the ostensible purpose of en-rapturing the occupants. I am very fond of music, but not when it's played *at* me, like an individually ad-dressed oration. To best appreciate the wandering restaurant violinist one must be drunk, or in love. Or both. I was neither, and "Sing, Gypsy, Sing" is not the ideal accompaniment for the assimilation of chef's salad and a TV idea. Therefore, when I saw the musical stroller coming in our direction, I lowered my head to the angle where my hat brim became a sheltering umbrella and conferred earnestly with the agent . . . a subterfuge which didn't in the least discourage the violinist who, having unfortunately finished his selec-tion, stood before our table, waiting for recognition, smiling, bowing and being eagerly Hungarian. I bowed back in a manner I hoped implied gracious dismissal, but he continued to hover and, as I feared he would, asked me to name my favorite tune. This has always struck me as being on a par of assininity with naming one's favorite color, in somebody's memory book. Moreover, a sudden question like that has a paralyzing effect on the mind and I can never think of anything but "Star Dust," which is actually not a particular favorite. Feeling slightly idiotic I named it. The ambu-lant maestro's bow swept out the opening bars while across the room, the remaining members of the quar-tette joined in with the mechanical ennui of performers who are constantly receiving requests for the same old piece from the same old country bumpkins.

I tried to pick up the business conversation, but it

was hard to discuss canned soup sponsors while someone was fiddling his heart out about a "melody that
haunts his reverie." I felt obliged to glance up occasionally at the virtuoso who, as he played, began to
gaze at us with fatuous knowingness. Apparently, in his
fantasy the agent and I must surely be recalling how
long ago we danced to these magic strains on our Ber-
muda honeymoon. Either that, or we had listened to
it coming over the radio of our clandestine love-nest.
In a horrified effort to correct such possible impres-
sions, I sat up straight and fixed him with a matter-of-
fact look. It was impossible to keep it fixed for he, by
now breathing heavily, was transfixed by a gaze of
ecstasy which, while inspired by his own playing, was
directed straight at myself and with such steady con-
centration, it seemed to give the further horrifying
impression that it was he rather than the agent with
whom I shared the love-nest. What does one do under
such circumstances? Gaze back? And if so, with what
expression? Responding ecstasy? Critical appraisal?
Eager appreciation? A dreamy stare at the ceiling, or
at the beads of perspiration on the man's brow might
have come in handy. And a way out would have been
the closed-eye coma of the music devotee, but this
wasn't Carnegie Hall and "Star Dust" doesn't rate it,
and in the meanwhile what would the agent be doing?
The unsatisfactory solution was to continue my conversation with him (he appeared to be having rather
a poor time himself), then, so as not to seem insensitive
to the musical treat, to glance up at the persistent min-

strel from time to time with bright little nods of approval.

I recall another time of similar discomfiture when, during a theatrical tour, I made the acquaintance of an attractive clergyman who, in a moment of vocational enthusiasm, asked if I'd give him my opinion on two or three of his sermons . . . a request which I, in a moment of mental derangement, agreed to do. I thought they'd be in the form of typewritten manuscripts which he'd drop by at the hotel and which at odd moments such as breakfast or the tub I could skim over casually enough to give the usual coherent lies. I was somewhat surprised when, the next afternoon, the phone rang and the clerical voice announced itself as being in the lobby and could it come up with the sermons; but when there was a discreet knock at the door and the gentleman appeared carrying a large machine and a small bag, I was thrown for a loop to discover that the machine was a dictaphone and the bag contained three sermons immortalized on cylinders. Listening while someone reads a script always makes me feel foolish, but that feeling is the essence of ease compared with my sense of assininity as I perched on a sofa holding to my ear the end of a hearing tube through which came the voice of the clergyman being his most inspired. It was very awful . . . especially as he, nervously smoking and pacing up and down the room, kept watching me intently. Again, where to look? Devoutly back at him? Or at the turning cylinder with equal devoutness? The awkwardness was not eased when every so often, in order to ascertain just what point we'd reached, he'd bend down and cup his ear within an inch of my own. Nor was it eased by the sermons which were very much the "yea verily" sort. To glance brightly up with smiling approval didn't seem sufficiently reverent, and yet, to listen with an expression of holy deadpan didn't seem right either. Release came at the final *amen* and I weakly protested that they were all just beautiful, for which prevarication I trusted a forgiving heaven to consider the pain of the situation sufficient punishment.

Fortunately such where-to-look situations do not arise with any frequency. One which does, however, is the elevator one . . . both while in an elevator and while waiting for one. The act of waiting for an elevator brings out a suspicious streak in people. You arrive before the closed landing door and push a button. Another person comes along and after a glance of mutual appraisal, you both look quickly away and continue to wait, thinking the while uncharitable thoughts of one another. The new arrival suspecting you of not having pushed the button and you wondering if the new arrival is going to be a mistrusting old meanie and go give the button a second shove . . . an unspoken tension which is broken by one or the other of you walking over and doing just that. Then back to positions of waiting and the problem of where to look. To stare the other person in the eye seems forward and usually the eye doesn't warrant it. Shoes are convenient articles for scrutiny—your own or those of the other person—although if overdone, this may give the impression of incipient shoe fetichism. Hotels, of course, often supply framed reading matter, but you can study such items as "Dance tonight in our Avo-cado Room to the Conga rhythms of Pepe Alvarez and his Poncho Gauchos" just so long before you're taken for one of those retarded adults with a reading defi-ciency. When there's no reading matter, the arrow of the indicator comes in for a lot of absorbed attention. Although this too has its annoyances. Like the watched pot, the watched arrow is reluctant to do its duty. It seems either to go into the slow motion of Big Ben's hour hand, or to stop fixed at a distant upper floor for so long you begin to think the operator is up to no good. Failing an arrow indicator, some people wait for the delivering glow of the Down light with the devotion of religious zealots waiting for the fiery chariot. When at last a light does go on and it proves to be the Up, disappointment is acute and the where-to-look problem continues. It continues even inside the elevator . . . especially in the crowded and claustro-phobic boxes of the modern high buildings. Any mu-tual exchange of glances on the part of the occupants would add almost a touch of lewdness to such already over-cozy sardine formation. Some people gaze instead at the back of the operator's neck, others stare trance-like up at those little lights which flash the floors, as if safety of the trip were dependent upon such deep con-centration.

A rather similar situation arises in a Pullman diner

when one is obliged to sit opposite an unknown at a table for two. How to fill in the awkward wait between writing out "Luncheon #4 with coffee" and the arrival and serving of same? If one is not the type who, given the slightest provocation, bursts into friendly chit-chat with a stranger, the risk of getting conversationally involved with someone who is, brings out the furtive behavior of an escaped convict. Sometimes it becomes apparent that the other person feels the same way . . . a discovery which comes as a minor shock but no major solution. Two strangers sitting directly opposite each other at a distance of a foot and a half and determined politely but firmly to avoid each other's eye, go in for a fascinating little game of "I don't spy." They re-read the menu, they fool with the cutlery, they inspect their own fingernails as if seeing them for the first time. Comes the inevitable moment when glances meet but they meet only to shoot instantly away and out the window for an intent view of the passing scene. Sometimes the scene isn't passing, being a station-stop closeup of a motionless freight car, in which case there is again some interesting reading matter such as A.T. & SF or *Route of the Zephyrs* or Westinghouse or, if one is mathematically inclined, whole series of numbers to have fun with.

Another looking problem *à deux* is when your dentist is bending over you and coming closer and closer with the intensity of Rudolph Valentino . . . only what he's after is not your soul but your cavity. To look back with responding intensity doesn't seem just right, and anyway who could pretend to be a second Vilma Banky with a mouth gaping open and wadded with a lot of little cotton bolsters? Moreover, by the time this Sheik of the bicuspid is going with light and pickaxe into the depths of the molar cavern, his face is at such immediate proximity, to look directly into his eyes means that your own will become crossed, while not to look means either closing yours, which might be considered curiously affected, or rolling them heavenward as when someone who has volunteered to extract a cinder approaches you with folded handkerchief and the command, "Look up!" The eye specialist settles the question by his own specific command of "Look straight at me." Only with him it's a question of where to breathe as, after plunging the room into darkness, he advances with lowered head as if to play "owl's eyes" and remains with you, brow to brow, for long moments of meditation. This weird session always rouses in me symptoms of minor hysteria. I have a girlish impulse to giggle, or to see what he'd do if suddenly I were to purse my lips and kiss him. Be it to the comfort of all eye specialists, I have up to now managed to keep such manic urges under control.

Then there is that situation when, after you've said good-bye to people, they keep turning up again. I am thinking specifically of shipboard acquaintances at the finish of an ocean voyage. Early in the morning as the ship noses into New York harbor, you and your lovely new friends the Smiths decide that what with the forthcoming confusion of landing and all, you'd better say good-bye right there and now. You exchange cards, telephone numbers, kisses, protestations about how wonderful it's been and extortions of promises that when next they come East, you must have a lot of get-togethers. It's a slight anticlimax when some minutes later, feeling it your duty to run out on deck and watch the Statue of Liberty go by, you discover that Mr. and Mrs. Smith, under similar patriotic compulsion, have turned up at the railing alongside. After some merry "well look who's here!"s and a few appropriate clichés about our Grand Old Girl, you repeat the good-byes, the "how wonderful it's been!"s and the promises to get together. This time, hearty handshakes replace the kisses and you take a second final farewell of your lovely new friends. A few minutes later you are summoned for health inspection and take your place in one of the two line-ups on either side of the upper Lounge. Directly across the room from you in the other line-up, are the Smiths. By now they don't seem so new and under the harsh light of the glass ceiling, they look much less lovely. The space between you and them is too wide to permit any exchange of conversation unless shouted, so you laughingly wave and go through certain assinine mouthing grimaces which nobody can possibly make out, but whose gist is what fun it's all been and how we must count on that get-together. Then after a final wave, you and the Smiths turn resolutely away to fix attention on the respective line-ups which are both at a halt, due in one case to a lady who has packed her vaccination certificate in her trunk in the hold and, in the other to a swollen-faced boy whose mother is explaining that it's a tooth and not the mumps. You try your best to avoid looking over at the Smiths who themselves seem to be aiming at similar avoidance, but every now and then, you involuntarily steal a furtive glance in their direction at the precise moment when they're doing the same thing and you feel obliged to engage in some more inane wavings and mouthings. The line-ups bring you and the Smiths simultaneously before the desk for inspection, after which formality you exchange a rapid "Well good-bye again," refrain from any mention of that get-together and almost knock each other down in a joint attempt to flee divergently.

Don't think, however, that you've seen the last of your lovely new friends. Everyone has overlooked the fact that their name begins with the same letter of the alphabet as yours and upon arrival on the dock there they are at the customs, their luggage within a few feet of your own. By now you're not only pretending you've never met, you're beginning earnestly to wish it were so—what's more you're making plans definitely to be out of town if ever they turn up for that get-together. And here you have a double where-to-look problem. There is something distressingly Peeping Tom-like about viewing the intimacies of anyone else's open trunks and suitcases. So now you must not only avoid looking at the Smiths, you must be careful to glance away as Mr. Smith's shaving brush inadvertently tumbles out of a case. It is a comfort to realize that when your own customs inspector opens a bag bursting with soiled underwear, some of which jams in the lock, the Smiths are tactfully absorbed in the contemplation of the ship's hawser.

If all the foregoing implies that I am one of those unpleasant shifties who can't look a fellow man in the eye, I have been grossly misleading. For no one is to me more irritating than the person who, when you're talking with him, keeps glancing off to one side as though looking for someone more interesting to come along, or possibly communing with some unseen spirit. And that in itself offers yet another where-to-look puzzler. Does one glance off to see what he's looking at, or continue talking to the side of his face, or would it help any to run around and place oneself in the focus of his vagrant attention?

As I said at the start, this supersensitivity may be a sign of neurosis. At least if it is, and if it gets bad enough for me to have to do something about it, there's comfort in the thought that the where-to-look problem won't arise on the analyst's couch. Maybe that's what the couches are there for. Maybe, and it's a cheery supposition, analysts themselves suffer from the same complaint.

Those Starring Days

Those Starring Days

ACTORS on tours seldom take the time to look at the front portions of whatever houses they play in, finding it more expedient to hurry to work down the worst-in-the-town alley and in through the almost un-discoverable stage door. On a recent one-night stand in the Northwest, I played in a theatre which, being a converted movie-house whose conversion was rather apostate, backed onto no alley and had no stage door. The only entry was through the front of the house. As I made my way across the outer lobby, I stopped dead in my tracks at the sight of an enormous hand-painted billboard heralding my impending appearance. Emblazoned on it also was a biographical digest of my life which read distressingly like an obituary notice. It began with my name, profession and place of birth, tactfully omitting the date . . . and then went on to list all the plays I had been in, even those dating back to my first years on the stage. What made this especially fascinating was the fact that it all came under a flaming red heading which read "STAR OF"!! Whoever had gathered this historical data must have done so from an ancient Who's Who. It must, in fact, have been gleaned from the edition which first included my name, a distinction I found so impressive at the time that in filling out the information blank I put down every production in which I had ever appeared or disappeared, and only a matter of space limit restrained me from including my triumphs in the Baldwin School Dramatic Club. Coming across these half forgotten titles was like opening a long neglected trunk and unpacking bits of the French lingerie you once thought was so lovely you had never had the heart to discard it . . . items with such nostalgic names as camisoles or teddy-bears . . . for to such an era belonged these early productions of which this placard billed me as having been the star. "Will Shakespeare," "Tweedles," "The Wild Westcotts," "In the Next Room" . . . As I stared at them a train of reminiscence took the place of astonishment in my mind.

My part (or parts) in "Will Shakespeare" was (or were) the first I ever landed on my own. The previous season my father had allowed me to try out my wings in his production of "Blood and Sand" and had then turned me loose to continue my theatrical flight without protection of the paternal net. For months I had worn out opera-pump leather along Broadway and in

the dingy waiting rooms of casting agencies. Thanks
to Father's name, managers would see me once . . .
but they seldom looked twice. Grotesquely thin and
gawky, I did my best to disguise a chronic shyness with
an appearance of world-weariness. This was effected
by a wardrobe of "outré" dresses most of which I myself concocted without benefit of sewing-machine and
without bothering to double the seams which occasionally furnished the chink in the armor of sophistication by coming unbasted. My hats were as near a
replica of Mistinguette's headgear as I and Macy's
trimming counter could devise. My posture was the
fashionable "slink" and for a facial expression I aped
Anita Stewart's . . . pouting rosebud mouth and eyebrows sweetly distressful like the two sides of an
accent circonflexe. The casual observer might have considered me, if not the femme fatale of my ambitions,
at least a mature eccentric, had not my voice betrayed
my callow years. I tried to keep it the throaty contralto
of Elsie Ferguson, but in moments of nervousness it
would go higher and higher until it ended in a bat-like
squeak.

After months of fruitless job-hunting, I got the break
of an interview with that prince of producers, Winthrop Ames. Having known the humiliations of incessant and often brusquely unpleasant turn-downs in
the offices I had haunted, it came as an agreeable shock
to encounter a delightful gentleman who, as I walked
in, actually rose, offered me a chair and enquired
charmingly about my family. In an access of nervous

pleasure, my voice began its upward ascent. I was determined Mr. Ames should not hear it in its high c squeak. What he did hear when politely he asked what type of acting I preferred was the tragedy thunder of a Sarah Siddons delivering the line "Mr. Ames, I hope eventually to play comedy." For a moment I believe he thought I was furnishing him with a sample of my talent, then my expression of dismay revealed my painful immaturity and with an amused but kindly smile he said he thought he could find a part for me in a production he was about to do of Clemence Dane's "Will Shakespeare."

He found me not one part but four. Those were the days before the entertainment unions had stipulated how many odd jobs an actor could take on and everybody doubled in brass . . . that is, everybody who was nobody. In the first scene, which took place in Shakespeare's Stratford cottage, I came on as a boy-player, a member of an Elizabethan road company. To establish the fact that we were strolling players we were first seen through a large window at the back, strolling. We were also singing. Then we came onto the stage, still strolling and singing. Ours was a song about London Towne whose effect upon the future Bard was to help entice him away from homespun pleasures and into the whirl of Tudor high-life. Of the incidental music Robert Benchley wrote:

"Deems Taylor has written some very catchy songs for them to sing in the tavern and around Stratford. But in common with all hey-nonny singers, they give the impression of having had glee club rehearsals every Tuesday and Thursday night since August to prepare for this one burst of spontaneous song. Perhaps the roisterers of the 16th Century were able to bound in and out of a bar-room with the first and second tenors and the first and second bases all hitting the opening note simultaneously, but it sounds suspiciously like something for which the secretary had sent out postcards urging every member to be present."

In this opening role, I said nothing. I merely wore tights, sang alto and tried to look terribly like a boy-player . . . while a short scene took place between Shakespeare and Henslow, the actor manager of our troupe who went through the gestures of offering the playwright a run-of-the-season contract. We then exeunted, still strolling and singing and once out of sight, I hurtled up three flights of iron stairs to a chorus dressing-room where I got into a trailing white garment for my next brief moment in which I was dimly discernible as another boy-player acting the feminine lead in an opening night performance of Romeo and Juliet. The set presented a behind-the-scenes view of the Globe Theatre with the play in process and nearing its conclusion. A door at the back led onto the supposed stage and when someone opened it for a second, I flitted past. My next moment was not even discernible, but it was at least periodically audible. I stood just outside that same on-stage door which Shakespeare, in a state of first night jitters, kept opening and closing. When he opened it, I spoke Juliet's lines. Actually they were meant to be spoken by Mary Fitton, who, according to the play, when the male ingénue cast as Juliet met with an accident, snatched off his costume, got into it herself and went on in his place for the Tomb Scene. (A rashling prank which stirred up quite a ruckus in court circles.) Due to the fact that Mary Fitton (beautifully played by Katharine Cornell) had a quick change to make, the while her voice had to be distantly heard, the voice they heard . . . distantly . . . was mine. At the end of the final line, I again hurtled . . . this time out through the wings and into a hallway where I madly applauded my own performance along with a group of the lesser members of the cast whose duty it was to give an effect of a London audience giving vent to feverish ovation. This sounds pretty confusing and I may say it was confusing to me too. After this clap-hands episode I again hurtled up three flights of iron stairs (actors when they get reminiscent always specify the ferrous quality of dressing-room stairs . . . probably to emphasize the rigors of their profession). There I changed into a court gown and headdress to appear in the final scene as maid-in-waiting to Queen Elizabeth, or Haidee Wright (the two will always be synonymous to me after watching the unforgettable acting of that tiny, wizened artist). At the Queen's bidding I waved from a casement to a primrose vendor in the street below, asked where she came from and, upon being told, remarked "Marlow's across the river, far from us," and that's as far as I "starred" in that show.

I had, nevertheless, a few unsung duties. At the dress

rehearsal Norman Bel Geddes and his then assistant Gerstle Mack used me as stand-in for the women of the cast in order to try out their lighting effects. I stood, sat, squatted and perched in and upon all visible areas of the set, trying to assume startlingly effective poses in the hope that Mr. Bel Geddes would notice my potentialities and insist at some future date upon having me in a show of his designing. The date is still in the future. I also understudied Katharine Cornell and Winnifred Lennihan in the respective roles of Mary Fitton, that Dark Lady of the Sonnets, and Ann Hathaway, or Mrs. Ann H. Shakespeare as she was during the action of the play. A youth named Charles Romano understudied both Otto Kruger as Will Shakespeare and Alan Birmingham as Kit Marlowe. What with four parts and all scenes between the two of us, our rehearsals were very active. Much of the time I spent either clinging desperately onto the young man's neck . . . he as Shakespeare, I as Ann; or perching wantonly upon his knee . . . I as Mary, he as both Shakespeare and Marlowe. I found both situations highly agreeable. The liveliest portion of our weekly session was when Romano as Shakespeare burst into a tavern to come upon himself as Marlowe and myself as Mary at an unusually flagrant moment of knee-perching, flew into dagger-drawing fury as Shakespeare at himself as Marlowe, leapt about the stage fighting himself in the mother and father of a brawl which ended with him as Marlowe falling onto a table edge and knocking himself dead and finally him as Shakespeare, staggering off in a well-justified daze.

The next show in which, according to that billboard, I "starred" was "Tweedles," a pleasant little comedy that could only have been written, and was, by Booth Tarkington. Its setting was a Cape Cod antique "shoppe" and the chief conflict of its genial plot was native pride as represented by the local family of Tweedles versus social snobbery as personified by some summer visitors named Baxter, with local integrity winning out and love, as embodied most charmingly in Ruth Gordon, a Tweedle, and Gregory Kelly, a Baxter, conquering all. I played a summer visitor . . . a "socialite" with a lot of money, a yen for young Baxter and the unfortunate name of Mrs. Ricketts. To any of my friends who had not seen the play, were not likely to and were considerate enough to enquire about my current part, I would modestly imply that I played the "menace." The menacing qualifications consisted in being referred to with lifted eyebrows as a divorcée, and in trying unsuccessfully to capture the amorous attentions of Gregory Kelly, my come-on being arch offers of drives in my open roadster which must surely have been a Stutz. A character more talked about than seen, I had only two brief scenes and, as I opened the play, all late comers, which meant half of any New York audience, missed the first one. At the rise of the curtain I came onto the antique shop set, called for the proprietress and enquired the price of certain items which I specified as being "quaint old" and at which I pointed with a black ivory-handled

cane. I forget now whether this exotic sartorial note
was the inspiration of myself or the management . . .
probably the latter, as I would have preferred a Tosca
staff. Then Ruth Gordon, winsome and wistful as
Winsora Tweedles, entered and we exchanged a few
lines which established Mrs. Ricketts as a highly unpleasant creature and Winsora as more wistfully winsome than ever. I then made an exit with snooty flourish
and for the remainder of the first act and the duration
of the second, sat in my dressing-room reading Stanislawski. Toward the middle of the last act, I came back
in a change of costume and a state of extreme agitation
over something that had to do with the local police,
a speeding ticket and that roadster. Donald Meek
played a comic Down East cop upon whom I vented
my wrath in a tirade which further established my
unpleasantness and added immeasurably to Mr. Meek's
comicness. Gregory Kelly once more turned down my
invitation for a ride, I made another snooty exit and
returned to Stanislawski until time for curtain calls of
which I participated in one . . . the first . . . a line-
up of the cast.

My next starring vehicle was something called "The
Wild Westcotts" about which I remember very little
except that it was meant to be frightfully madcap. It
involved an endearingly demented family, a farcical
cook, a society lady, an English captain and a number
of guests. There was a lot of door banging, shouting,
colliding, double-taking and some good clean fun over
the audacity of a young girl saying "DAMN!" Elliott

Nugent played an inarticulate youth in love with Vivian Martin who was in love with the English captain who, in turn, was in love with . . . of all people . . . me. My role was again that of a "socialite" and again it was more talked about than talking, but it at least had the dazzling name of Geraldine Fairmont and my British suitor was none other than one Captain Hippesley Trenchard. What was more, it brought me in my first press notice which said that the part was "nicely acted and beautifully dressed." The critic was Charles Belmont Davis, a good friend of the family. Albeit I would have preferred to have seen the adverbs reversed, the review, I felt, warranted the purchase of a tooled leather scrap book. Still dedicated to Stanislawski, I did my best to *live* my part, bringing to it the sultriness of Olga Petrova, the worldly chic of Mrs. Lydig Hoyt and my lovable Anita Stewart expression. My characterization was lost on the director who during a break in the dress rehearsal called out to me for the love of Mike to stop making that face. I shared a dressing-room with Claudette Colbert whose position in the cast was even lower than mine. At the finish of the brief run, she received a movie offer and I received a prospectus from the Fagan School of Dramatic Art.

Of these early "starring" productions the one I best recall was a detective melodrama in which I played only during the out-of-town try-out and the closing weeks most of which were semi out-of-town for they were spent on the subway circuit. Again under the elegant aegis of Winthrop Ames the play "In the Next Room" was an adaptation by Mrs. August Belmont and Harriet Ford of Burton S. Stevenson's "Mystery of the Boule Cabinet." It was a first-rate thriller, complete with chills, face-at-the-window, corpses and a detective who turns out to be . . . you're right . . . the criminal. An unusual twist to the who-done-it formula was that the killer was not a who, but a what, for the murders were committed by an 18th Century cabinet . . . that is, by a poisoned fang connected to a secret drawer cleverly concealed on the left hand side. This drawer harbored the "world famous Mazarin diamonds" and anyone who went monkeying around with the hidden springs was liable to be nailed by the deadly gadget. On the right hand side of the homicidal antique was another secret cubicle in which unbeknown to the jewel-thieves were hidden the love-letters of a certain Duchesse de Charrière, an American heiress wed to a cruel nobleman who had recently killed her lover in a duel and was hot after the letters as evidence for divorce. The Duchesse was hot after them too and determined to get them first as she wished to avoid the scandal of a divorce (this was still somewhat the age of innocence).

I played the Duchesse. When Ames offered me the role, I accepted with eager rapture. My mother's emotions were more mixed. The prospect of my playing a femme-du-monde who had had an illicit love affair gave her pause for thought. But then, as she said, this Moscow Art cult about "living one's part" need not be taken too literally (not that I wouldn't have jumped at the chance to do so) and besides Mr. Ames was such a gentleman and so was the director that nice Mr. McClintic and Mary Kennedy the leading lady was such a bright young woman and she thought it would be pleasant if some afternoon I'd ask them all up to tea.

We opened in Atlantic City. It was a week filled with instructive surprises. One thing I learned was that in a detective show anything can go wrong and the audience accepts it as being part of the plot. The intense action of the play necessitated a number of blackouts and these in turn necessitated some speedy and pretty hectic scene and furniture shifting. During one of these scrambling changes, a stagehand, bewildered in the dark, found himself caught on the set when the lights went up. Rather than make a conspicuous exit, he ducked down behind a large sofa and remained there cramped and motionless for the rest of the act. At first no one noticed him except the members of the cast who when they met up with him were thrown for a loop. Then certain occupants of the gallery from their bird's-eye vantage point became aware of the crouching form and a horror stricken hiss of "There's someone behind the sofa! There's someone behind the sofa!" communicated itself on down to the balcony and eventually to the entire house who waited in a state of pleasurable terror for Sammy the assistant carpenter to leap up and strangle someone. The fact that the identity of this sinister figure was never clarified bothered no one in the least.

Those secret drawers furnished a certain amount of lively confusion. They were simulated by tiny hinged panels which on certain cues mysteriously opened. These were worked by means of strings fastened to screw-eyes on the inside of the panels and carried on out through holes in both the cabinet and the scenery wall. The flaps were set at an angle so that when the strings went slack, they would flop down. This simple mechanism was the inspired invention of the property man who sat backstage holding the strings taut. When the cues came, he'd release one or the other string and the aperture would appear. The first secret cubicle to be revealed was the one containing the Duchesse's guilty love-letters. It was I who supposedly demonstrated the combination, going through the gestures of working a series of hidden springs the while I explained "First I press here, then here, then here," and the rest of the cast watched with frozen tension. The third *here* was the property man's cue for letting go the string, the panel shooting open and the cast reacting with appropriate gestures of amazement. One rainy night in Atlantic City, I went through the usual business, spoke the cue lines and stood back for the revelation of the cubicle. Nothing happened. Thinking that perhaps the property man had failed to hear me, I repeated my press here, then here, then here formula in a slightly louder tone. Nothing continued to happen. Finally in desperation and the voice of a commander during battle, I bellowed "First I press here, then here, then *HERE!!!*" and at that there came from backstage the equally desperate voice of the property man shouting "Shake it!" Dampness had caused the wood to swell and the flap was stuck motionless. The tense immobility of the cast was starting to thaw to nervous restlessness. I clawed frantically at the crack of the aperture and as a last resort, was about to pry it loose with a hairpin when like the lid of a jack-in-the-box, it shot open. The packet of love-letters shot with it and fell at my feet. Claude King who played the detective and I stooped in unison to pick it up with a nice precision that brought our heads together in a sharp whack that almost finished the play for both of us.

On another occasion the capricious flaps went into reverse disorder. My safe-cracking, or rather cabinet-cracking bit of business was preceded by a long speech in which I gave a highly emotional account of my unhappy marriage, the duel between my husband and lover, the death of the latter and a desperate request that I be allowed to salvage the letters. (How they had gotten into the cabinet in the first place and then made the trip from Paris to Gramercy Square is a facet of the plot that escapes my memory.) The speech was my big moment. It was, in fact, a number of them, for it lasted a good two and a half minutes and I gave it whatever was my all. I was therefore quite discouraged one evening when as I started addressing the first portion of it to Claude King, to see that gentleman turn away and walk deliberately off the stage through a door at the back. I then addressed myself to the young man playing the reporter and was further discouraged and equally bewildered when he made an exit right. Mary Kennedy, the leading lady, was seated on the sofa and when I tried to engage her interest in my moving story, she rose, muttered "Excuse me" and went off left. The only person remaining on stage was a psychopathic footman. He was standing as far away from me as the set would permit, in a state of partial coma. For lack of any other listener, I told my life story to him. His only reaction was to stay on in his coma. At the finish of my enforced monologue, the three missing members of the cast returned as inexplicably as they had departed. It was not till later than I learned that as I came on for my scene, the panel of secret drawer no. 2 (the one of the poison fang and the Mazarin diamonds) flopped open. Each of the three saw it happen, each realized that if the audience noticed it the plot would be ruined and each had the bright idea of slipping quietly out during my solo narrative to tell the property man for God's sake to haul up the string. What the audience thought of this strange action is not known any more than whether they made head or tail of the still stranger action which followed immediately. The bluff, florid Englishman playing the butler was waiting in the wings for a later entrance in which he ran on with a glass of water to resuscitate a fainting parlor maid. Suddenly seeing the three members of the cast come off, and thinking he had missed his cue, he grabbed up the glass and tore onstage several minutes ahead of time, looked wildly around for the parlor maid who had not as yet appeared, spluttered a loud

"Beg pardon, Sir" to nobody in particular and tore off again. As I mentioned before, in a mystery play, anything can happen . . . and does.

My nostalgic reverie was cut short by the local manager, who came up to find out how I liked the billboard. Before I could answer he asked, "What was it like starring in all those plays?" I spluttered, "Well, I'll tell you. . . ." Then I thought better of it, looked at my watch and told him the time instead, and rushed off to my dressing room leaving him to his own conjectures.

Storming the Barns

Storming the Barns

THE cheery ads in the papers of the summer theatres optimistically preparing to launch their precarious seasons, have set me reminiscing somewhat nostalgically about certain personal experiences in the straw-hat belt. In my own daylight-saving time, I have known quite a few of these establishments at first hand. . . . There have been playhouses with audiences composed of knowledgeable theatre-goers and others whose patrons, glowing with suntan oil and yacht-club liquor, saunter in without any idea of whether they're going to see *The Cherry Orchard* or *A Tree Grows in Brooklyn,* regarding any show as merely a stop-gap between coffee and canasta.

Everyone takes summer theatre in whatever is one's stride. Maybe the fact that most of them are located in or near resorts prevents actor and public from taking them with undue tension. It is hard to be professionally dedicated when the resident company turns up for first reading in wet bathing suits or when your nontheatrical friends who are "just motoring through" drop by the box-office and suggest that you knock it all off and go out with them for a little drink. Then too, there is an offstage rapport between company and public . . . which gives a sense of the pleasantly casual. Summer residents seem eager to meet summer actors, and summer actors often seem quite eager to be met, especially when it leads to a certain amount of free food and drink. There is something rather disarming about those lay persons who want to find out "what actors are like."

I recall furthering such research for some socially eminent Long Islanders when I was serving theatrical time in a North Shore barn. It actually was a barn, situated bang against the railroad bank and our entr'acts had to be timed to coincide with the whooping passage of the Shoreham express. A nearby hostess whom I knew casually, called me at the box-office to say she was coming with guests to the show that evening and wouldn't I bring the cast to her place for supper afterward. She had some friends, she said, who would be so interested in meeting actors in the flesh. It sounded rather like a nudist invitation but I relayed it to the rest of the company who, tired of the midnight provender of the local Greasy Spoon, accepted with alacrity. After the show, we drove to the lady's elegant place, and entered a room crowded with people in

evening clothes and if they were curious to find out
what actors were like, a first glance told them what
they weren't, and that was like their soigné'd selves.
The invitation having arrived just prior to curtain
time, we wore our everyday attire, that motley peculiar to summering actors, which has an eye to the
picturesque and economical. This, however, was what
seemed expected. One of the lady guests, a-glitter with
jewels, whispered the word "bohemian" to somebody
and one felt that her evening was made. It may have
been made, but it was far from over, either for her or
for a young Englishman in our corps whom I shall call
Martin.

Any awkward sense on the part of the hosts that
they might have let in the wrong people, or on the
part of the actors that they didn't belong, was dispelled
by that quick leveler of caste, drink. The socially
prominents had already reached a certain alcoholic
elevation and it took no time for us "rogues and vaga-
bonds" to attain their altitude. In the case of Martin,
a skilled alpinist in such matters, he outdistanced us
all and, as the evening progressed, appeared to be aiming for Everest. Martin was a British zany with a fund
of stories so Hogarthianly raw, only a charming English actor could have gotten away with them. When
he started in on the first, I fumbled with clammy hands
for my car-key, certain we'd be asked to leave. But
again, this was in line with what was expected and for
over an hour, Martin with charm and impeccable dic-
tion went through his shameless repertory to an audi-

ence that gasped, blushed, guffawed, howled and all but rolled on the floor. It was like a scene from Congreve in the windows of Kohler of Kohler. The lady who had whispered "bohemian" listened with fascination. She seemed scarcely to believe that such a person could exist. Hers was the happy amazement of the Prince discovering the golden nature of the Pauper. She followed him around all evening and when the party broke up and she learned that he was living in a Manhasset lodginghouse, she insisted that he go back with her and her husband to their place for what remained of the night. Martin was in no condition to resist, and within a few minutes he found himself lolling against the grey upholstery of a Rolls, flanked on one side by Mrs. Millions who kept talking about how fascinating an actor's life must be, and, on the other, by Mr. Millions who kept silent but was obviously leery of the fascination.

The big limousine wound about the lush Westbury lanes. Martin, equally lush, was off in a little world of his own. All at once he came to, yet still in what he took for a dream-world as they passed through wrought-iron gates, along a box-bordered drive, pulled up before a Tudor portico and entered a vast Hampton Courtly hall. With valiant effort, Martin summoned up his best English gentleman manner and wove with dignity after his hostess down a tiled corridor and into a lavish guestroom where, after donning a pair of silk pyjamas grimly furnished by his host, he fell into bed and drifted off under the happy illusion that he was

Henry VIII at the apex of his glory. Some seven hours later, he woke with the bleak disillusionment that he was Martin the Only at the depth of his misery, and with the sense of a presence in the room. The presence was an alarmingly elegant manservant who was standing at the foot of his bed in the attitude of an interne watching a patient emerge from ether. Martin sat up and croaked out a greeting of sorts to which the manservant responded with a frigid bow and the information that it was nearly noon, sir, his bath was drawn, sir, and luncheon would be at one. The realization that he had a matinée came as one more split to Martin's excruciated head.

The footman went out and Martin availed himself of the bath and, quaveringly, of some shaving equipment, an effort which sent him back to bed for a few minutes' recuperation. The footman came in with a silver tray containing orange juice, coffee, an Alka-Seltzer tablet and a vase with a single rose. Martin gratefully partook of the first three and politely sniffed the rose while the man busied himself setting out the actor's wildly unmatching jacket and pants as well as his shirt and shorts, which appeared, miraculously, to have been freshly laundered. The footman re-exited and immediately re-entered with another silver tray . . . the sort bellboys use, only instead of telegram or special delivery, it bore a pair of brand new socks. "Modom's compliments," he said, "Yours had holes in them." Martin blushed prettily and buried his nose in the rose. The footman left and Martin managed to shake himself into his exquisitely valeted garments not eased by the thought that payday wasn't till tomorrow and he hadn't a penny for tips. The footman returned with a generous whiskey sour and the explanation that Modom had found one of these highly beneficial. Leaving the actor to similar benefit, he again went out and again returned, this time with a telephone which he plugged into a wall socket, picked up and proffered the receiver and said that Modom had thought he might care to phone his mother in England. Dimly Martin recalled during his Himalayan elevation of the night before, having made mention of his dear little English mother, but the prospect of putting in an overseas call to her scared even the hangover out of him. The old lady lived in a tiny Wessex hamlet where the only telephone was at the tobacconist's and he knew that if she were summoned to speak over it, the poor soul would probably suffer a heart attack. For a moment he toyed with the notion of calling one of his less homespun female acquaintances in London; but that didn't seem quite practical as, with the footman hanging around, he'd be forced to address her as "Mother." He murmured something about his mother being away for the grouse season, finished off the whiskey sour and went in search of Modom whom he found on a terrace downing her second beneficial booster. She wanly urged him to do the same. The benefit for both was imperceptible.

Mr. Millions made a majestic, if not too happy appearance, turned aside a whiskey sour with the pious gesture of St. Anthony dismissing an especially revolting temptation and said, a bit pontifically, that he was counting on golf to do the trick. Luncheon was a bleak affair. The enchantment of the previous evening was not to be recaptured. Martin made sporadic attempts to be amusing to which Mrs. Millions responded as to the bright sayings of a Quiz Kid who was getting on everyone's nerves. The life of the actor seemed much less fascinating to both of them and even less so to Martin when, an hour later, he showed up for the matinée with eyes like carnations and hands like the quaking aspen. It was perhaps just as well that the rest of us didn't feel so good either. It made it easier to be lenient with Martin when, during a scene involving some tea-drinking, he inadvertently shot a cup into the wings.

Interest in actors is not always as genial as that of this hospitable Long Island coterie. In New England's summer climes, the attitudes of the seasonal residents is apt to be one of dark suspicion. At least I found it so one year when, doing a stint at a Maine resort, I committed the error of putting up, not in the pleasant boarding-house with the rest of the company, but in one of those highly inflammable frame-and-shingle chateaux which for decades has catered to the same clientèle. Elderly ladies, for the most part, as stern and rockbound as the coastal view, a sort of terrifying sisterhood in uniforms of chiffon print, white felt hats and nurse's shoes. The arrival of anyone not a member of their order was in the nature of an intrusion and when it was bruited about that *an actress* was in their midst, their reaction was such that I felt that my uniform should be a duplicate of Hester Prynne's after she got her scarlet letter. To be sure, I encountered them chiefly at meal time.

The first evening, as I meekly followed the lady head-waiter to my allotted table which, most awkwardly, was located at the distant end of the bleak, uncarpeted diningroom, I proved to be an object of interest greater even than the relish-tray and far less welcome. Resort ladies, when they recognize someone they've seen in the theatre, do one of two things, either they beam, or they glare. These were glarers. I made up my mind, that by the end of my stay, I'd convert them into beamers . . . less from motives of vindicating the profession than with an eye to the Saturday matinée (I was playing on a percentage). All the first week, I stuck carefully to the rules of local Hoyle. At every meal, I exchanged glad weather comments with the hostess, I told the waitress that I was just fine, thanks, and how was *she?* I listened earnestly to the hot-bread-boy's report on the temperature of the water and I leapt to my feet to gaze seaward with splendid animation whenever anyone said "Look! A seal." By Friday, the regulars appeared to be resigned to my presence and one or two glarers had actually turned into beamers.

The play was *Romance*, Edward Sheldon's enchantingly hearts-and-flowers opus about an Italian opera diva and a young clergyman, a setting of New York

in the '6o's with every delicious tear-jerking device
from the *Mignon* aria to sleighbells and choir voices
on New Year's Eve. The role of the singer La Cavallini,
complete with accent, Traviata costumes, sinful past
and hopeless love, is an actress' dream. One fascinating
facet of the glittering part is a scene in which she enters
the clergyman's study, carrying a muff on which is
perched a live monkey whom, in a naughty dig at her
operatic rival, she calls Adelina Patti. My contract
called for me to furnish my own costumes while the
management supplied the monkey.

Studying my lines at home, I had given little thought
to the monkey. As I drove to first rehearsal, it occurred
to me that my familiarity with the species was a nod-
ding acquaintance from barrier to cage in the Central
Park zoo. On arrival backstage, I was met by a youth
who told me that he was in charge of Adelina. "She's
just bitten Brenda" he said brightly, then added,
"Would you like to try her?" . . . for size or bite he
didn't specify. Looking toward where he pointed, I
identified Brenda, holding out a punctured forefinger
on which a lad familiar with First Aid (there's one
in every company) was daubing iodine. They were
both being terribly sporting about it. I was glad they
were each too young to have known about that king
of Greece who died from a monkey-bite and rather
sorry I wasn't.

Apprehensively I went through the formalities of
being introduced to Adelina who was handed to me
on the end of a leash. Adelina was the variety known

as a green monkey, which means that she was completely grey. Strange to say, she and I got along very well right from the start. To be sure, we didn't see much of one another, for our joint scene was very short. Holding her by the leash, I brought her in on my muff, spoke the sly comment about her resemblance to the immortal Patti, then lest she steal the act, handed her, along with the muff, to a servant who exited in fitting indignation. During rehearsals, Adelina behaved quite docilely during her brief appearance, seldom making any more disturbance than the utterance of a few bird-like chirps or occasionally the casting of herself off from the muff to hang upsidedown on the end of the leash, lost in troubled thought. In fact, Adelina seemed to be the least of our worries.

The choice of *Romance*, a play with a large cast and three solid sets is indicative of the slap-happy optimism of summer stock. The first scene was laid in a plush and ormolu Fifth Avenue mansion during a grand old New York ball. At the back was a marble staircase (constructed of plywood) and up and down this, at given moments between waltz records, extras representing the élite of Gotham tripped (the verb was occasionally apposite), ad-libbing softly and letting out those frighteningly giddy laughs peculiar to extras. The students of the Drama School were impressed for these members of the beau monde. They rehearsed in shorts and bare feet.

The night of the dress rehearsal a crisis arose from the fact that whoever had hired the men's dress suits had neglected to think of pumps and the elegant dandies wandered forlornly through their paces in swallow-tails, ruffled shirts and those same bare feet. Then there was a scene in which I as the notorious singer and Donald Cook as the pure young clergyman (yes, honest!) seated appropriately on a love-seat, became overcome with guilty passion and swooned into one another's arms . . . only what made us swoon was not passion guilty or innocent, but a horrendous stink which proved to be the presence of a dead mouse in the love-seat.

The worst crisis, however, was Adelina. The lights drove her wild with terror and from being the docile organ-grinder pet she had been during rehearsals, she became a raging Gargantua. She chattered, she screamed. She scooted onto my shoulder, wound her tail about my neck, bit my chin, snatched off my earrings, yanked out my Offenbach ringlets, let out whooping whistles and committed misdemeanors beyond the remedial powers of the local drycleaners. It was clear there'd be no taming her in time for the next day's opening. It was the consensus of opinion that a smaller monkey would wreak less havoc. Someone suggested a capuchin and, there being no pet shop within a radius of a hundred miles, I volunteered to wire my husband who was flying up for the opening, to bring one along.

The dress rehearsal ended at eight in the morning. I staggered back to my room in the wooden chateau, pausing first to dispatch the telegram over a Western

Union coin-box situated in the outer lobby and within earshot of the verandah which even at that early hour held a number of the stern and rocker-bound brigade. After I'd hung up I realized that they had listened happily to every word of the message which read:

"Local Adelina too big and savage. Bring me a small and kindly female capuchin. Also this county is dry."

It was the "female capuchin" which had them stymied. Someone muttered "nuns" and that evening as I downed an early supper before the show, the entire dining-room watched me with beady speculation. It was the arrival of my husband which justified their zeal. Preceded by a flustered hostess, he made a har-assed entrance down the length of the dining-room, bearing two paper-wrapped bundles which he dumped into my lap saying at the top of his voice (and it was a considerable top) "What won't you ask me to do next! That's your whiskey and the other's a jar of live grubs for your goddam Adelina. There weren't any capuchins so I brought a marmoset. It's outside with my bags." Then, after a double take around the room and its stunned occupants, he added in loud-speaker *sotto voce* "Holy God! Who are all these old bid-dies?" . . . only "biddies" was not what he said.

The new Adelina proved to be a weird little beastie with a fuzzy body, a chenille tail and a head like a mini-ature of Horace Greeley in blackface. She was easy to handle . . . which meant that when she bit, she didn't break the skin. During her act, she behaved with decorum, sitting quietly on my muff in which she searched gravely for possible succulent vermin. Her chief drawback was that her minute size prevented a large portion of the audience from determining what she was. Some thought she was a baby raccoon, others a chipmunk and one myopic acquaintance congratulated me on my trained praying mantis.

Alas, little Adelina the Second's career was pitifully brief. The Maine climate proved too rugged for her equatorial constitution. Friday night she lay limp and shaking on the muff and a few hours later, breathed her tiny last. The immediate problem was how to acquire a new Adelina in time for the matinée. Actually, as far as plot went, there was no vital reason for the pet to be a monkey. Donald Cook and his wife volunteered the loan of their dog . . . an old-fashioned pug with a corkscrew tail and a nose so Victorian, the animal was practically incapable of breathing. It was perfect as far as period went. When it came to gender, that was another matter, for this was a sturdy little male, and defiantly so, in the shameless manner of short-haired dogs. As a gesture of emasculation, we tied a pink bow about his small bull-like neck and I counted on deft handling of the muff and a bunch of Parma violets to conceal further evidences of miscasting. The dog completely loathed these indignities. Instead of sitting up sprucely he sprawled heavily all over the muff in an attitude of wretched embarrassment. His head and legs kept oozing slowly off and having to be scooped back. It was like handling a lethargically animated sandbag. At the moment in which I pointed out the resemblance to Adelina Patti, the creature started sliding to the floor. I made a grab which caught him from behind by the front paws and, as I spoke the line, he hung like a quartered veal in a butcher shop, as blatant as an anatomy chart, before an audience largely composed of my hotel ladies. As one of them was heard to remark in shocked tones "It just goes to show."

The first Adelina was not to be readily dismissed from my life. A local press-agent and his wife adopted her, rechristened her Cornelia Otis Skinner Grossmann, taught her some circus tricks which were publicized in rural papers and for years, through my zealous clipping bureau, I received her press notices . . . and at 10¢ apiece!

One summer I allowed my son to be exposed to summer stock. At the veteran age of nine he made his appearance with me in "Madame Sans-Gêne." This was Sardou's piece about a brash Paris laundress who becomes the Duchess of Danzig and horrifies the Napoleonic court with her uncouth manners . . . all very plush and spectacular and full of those theatricals which Shaw dismissed as "Sardoodledums." The first act takes place during the French Revolution when the Little Corporal hasn't the wherewithal to pay for his clean shirts and the big scene, set some fifteen years later, is when Napoleon, at the height of his power and trying to oust Sans-Gêne from the Tuilleries, is confronted by her with his unpaid laundry bill. My son pleaded and nagged to be allowed to go on in the first scene as part of the revolutionary mob and I, thinking it would be rather darling, fatuously agreed.

He was costumed and made up by the extras whose dressing-room he shared and a more gory revolutionary never stormed a barricade. In torn shirt, red-paint spattered trousers and, what was his chief delight, a kerchief drenched with lipstick tied over one eye, he rushed on with the mob at the start of the play, ran off with them crying "Down with" whatever it was, and then was seen no more . . . supposedly. However, he was so pleased with himself that nothing would induce him to get out of his costume before the final curtain. Such dedication seemed to me quite sweet until one matinée day when, during the big moment in Napoleon's study, Brandon Peters, who was playing the Emperor, whispered in my ear, "Look in the fireplace!" There, between the 1810 eagle-crested andirons, was the face of a young 1790 revolutionary, watching our goings-on with shining eyes. For a moment, Brandon Peters and I stood transfixed. The stage manager who didn't see what had happened, thought we had dried up and threw us a line. My small revolutionary moved forward to get a better view. Brandon started to break up and Napoleon's scowl turned into a broad grin. My son took this for a bit of high comedy and shook with gleeful appreciation. Again he moved further out into the fireplace. By now he was plainly visible to at least a third of the audience some of whom, I learned later, thought him part of the plot . . . possibly an assassin dispatched to kill the emperor. I made a waving gesture at him to get back. He responded with a polite wave of his own. Turning my back to the audience, I made what I hoped was a frighteningly reprimanding face at him. He took this for pure slapstick farce and put his hand over his mouth to suppress explosions of appreciative laughter. He also moved further out. It was Brandon Peters who solved the situation by saying, "If you'll pardon me, Madame, I must have a word with my equerry," striding out into the wings long enough to advise the stage manager, and two seconds later the young Spirit of the French Revolution was yanked back by the seat of his torn pants. After the curtain I called him to my dressing-room and gave him the mother and father of a dressing-down. Sarah Siddons' tones, which caused the linen draper to faint, were as nothing to my tirade at my offspring. Who did he think he was, just because he was the son of the star, what gave him the right to hang around the stage, he a lowly extra not even getting a salary, had ruined the scene, disgraced the family name, he must go immediately and apologize to everyone in the company for such outrageous behavior. He turned a little pallid under the gory make-up and went out.

We both kept silent, as later we drove back to the hotel for supper between shows. I went to my room to freshen up. My nine-year-old went to his. When I called him for dinner, there was no response. I opened his door and found him stretched on the bed, his head buried in the pillow, sobbing out the hurt of his first theatrical heartbreak. "It's all right, son," I said, "you've had your first flop. There'll be plenty of others and you'll never get used to them," and to keep from sobbing along with him, I got a wet towel, cleaned his face and slicked up his hair. As he went in to supper he said, "But Ma, I didn't think *anything* mattered in summer stock." To which I found myself replying, "I think perhaps you've got something there, fellow. Hurry up, Toots, we've got a show to do tonight."

Crying in the Dark

Crying in the Dark

Gene Lockhart once wrote a song called "Let's All Have A Good Cry" which expressed to a nicety the truism that there's no telling what human beings will consider as coming under the heading of entertainment. One of the most incongruous facets of the nature of *homo* not so *sapiens* is the delight with which he wallows in temporary orgies of utter misery. This was brought home to me the other day when, with swollen eyes, polished nose and dankly shredded Kleenex, I emerged into the harsh glare of daylight saving after seeing the revival of Charlie Chaplin's *City Lights*. As I went down the street still dripping like a freshly turned off garden whirligig, a passing acquaintance stopped me to enquire with gentle tact if anything serious were the matter, to which I replied with a happy sob: "Oh no. I've just had the most wonderful time at a heartbreaking movie!"

I first became acutely aware of this anomalous form of enjoyment when, as a gangly monstrosity of fifteen,

I was taken with a group of schoolmates by our teacher of that subject which is now called "Speech" but which in those days went by the ambiguous name of "Articulation" to attend a matinée of *Peter Ibbetson*. I was at the time going through a period of adolescent awfulness in which I tried to appear pale, interesting and world-weary (the popular term was blasé) and incapable of any reaction to sentiment unless possibly that expressed in the novels of Elinor Glynn which, being strictly forbidden, I read omnivorously. I also tried to appear a dead ringer for Theda Bara. This ambitious objective called for gobs of mascara and as that too was strictly forbidden I had to wait until I was well away from home before applying it. The *Peter Ibbetson* I saw was the poetically lovely Barrymore production, with John as Peter, Lionel as Colonel Ibbetson and Constance Collier the Duchess of Towers. At Peter's touching encounter with the broken and aging Major Duquesnois I started to shed my sophistication, at the first dream sequence when, transported to the Passy garden, he beholds himself as the child Gogo and the Duchess as little Mimsey Seraskier, my mascara started flowing after the sophistication and by the time the elderly lovers were voicing their farewells on the park bench in Auteuil, I buried my face on the shoulder of the Articulation teacher beside me and blubbered: "You tell me what's happening! I can't look!" The next time I recall similar crying in the dark was over that tender classic *L'Arlesienne* as produced at the Paris Odéon. This time my seat was next to that of an unknown elderly Frenchman who in emotional display outdid even myself and who was so overcome at one point that he suddenly grabbed my hand, shook it vigorously and said that evidament this was a ridiculous play but did it not do one of good sometimes to enjoy a little sentiment and ma foi what could one find to weep over in a tragedy of Corneille except perhaps the length of the acts?

The old boy summed up the average playgoer's reactions to a nicety because obviously what makes us weep is that happy combination of good theatre and good pathos known in the colorful language of Broadway as "schmaltz." Tragedy can break the heart but not the dam of the tearducts while schmaltz can dissolve the most hardened sophisticate. Tristan and Isolde can expire at the Met season after season without the audience extracting a handkerchief except maybe to muffle a sneeze caused by the dust from that venerable bear-rug; but the moment Mimi and Rudolfo start their candle searching, a trumpet voluntary of blown noses starts competition with the music. Gian-Carlo Menotti's *Consul* moved me so I, like the heroine, wanted to place my head in the first available oven and turn on the gas, but I shed no tear, whereas when the gentle "umfundisi" of *Lost in the Stars* told his grandson about the little house which wasn't much to sing about but was home, I choked up so audibly the people in front of me said "Sh!"

Looking back over my years as a happy theatre

sobber, I think what has moved me has been less the play itself than the specific moment in the play. That poignant moment, for instance, in Drinkwater's *Abraham Lincoln* when Frank McGlynn as the gaunt man of sorrows turned upstage to face a large map of the country and in the agonized gesture of the Crucified, stretched out his arms across the Union he was trying so desperately to save. There was the moment at the finale of *Porgy* . . . the non-musical one and also the subsequent Gershwin version when the crippled Porgy hunched himself into his little goat-cart and started off with childlike faith from Catfish Row in search of his Bess. And there was another moment in another Negro classic when de Lawd leaves his *Green Pastures* to visit Noah who entertains him unaware until a clap of thunder reveals the Presence and Noah, shaken but beatified, stands with bowed head and says: "I should have known you, Lawd, I should have seen the glory!" There was the moment hardly to be borne in *Journey's End* when Leon Quartermaine as the gentle, scholarly major who loves Alice in Wonderland and rock gardening, is picked out to be one of the raiding party due to go over the top to almost certain death, quietly remarks: "Excuse me. I have some letters to write." The moment when Elizabeth Barrett said her silent farewell to the house of Wimpole Street. The many moments of beauty during Frank Craven's genially simple and tenderly homespun account of the happenings in *Our Town*. And there was the moment when the curtain fell slowly to the wailing tune played by an

Arab on a "sweet potato" in Saroyan's zanily glorious bar where was to be found *The Time of Your Life.* Their very recollection can still start in my throat a rapidly rising lump.

In addition to dramatic situations there are certain players to whom I am tearfully allergic the way some people are to certain composers—players whose most casual speech as far as my reactions go might be the Death of Little Nell. Helen Hayes could come out with "How's your foot?" and I'd weep softly. When, however, as *Victoria Regina,* after Disraeli has drunk the toast, broken the glass and taken his last leave she comes out with "Such devotion! Most extraordinary!" and then that cry of the heart—"Oh Albert! Albert!" —the soft weeping turns into muffled bawling. And while we are on Victorian lines, I wonder how many of us remained dry-eyed at *Cavalcade* when the Queen's coffin passed beneath the window and the small boy remarked: "Mummy, she must have been a very little lady!"

It is not always the "schmaltzy" moment which dissolves us. Sometimes it's a mere mannerism or attribute. The poetry of Duse's hands, the melodious catch in Ethel Barrymore's voice, the burning nobility of Olivier's eyes, the eloquence of Katharine Cornell's quickly raised throat, the damp handkerchief of Jane Cowl and even when it was dampened by the treacle of such an opus as *Smilin' Through.* Such characteristics which are as much a part of the specific actor as the brush-stroke is a part of the specific painter.

We like our players to be characteristic of themselves. The anticipated appearance of a well-loved star, looking as we've hoped he or she will look—only more so—rouses in us the same sort of breath-catching emotion experienced by the devotionally wide-eyed tourist when he first comes upon Notre Dame—looking exactly like Notre Dame, only more so. When, after an absence of far too many years, Maurice Chevalier, complete with straw hat and world-embracing grin, sauntered out before a New York audience to a musical flurry of *Valentine*, I wanted to cheer, shout the *Marseillaise* and kiss the stranger on my right—but instead, I gave vent to such nostalgic tears my son, who was on my left and profoundly mortified, instantly pretended to be a stranger too. The grand old performer strutting his grand old stuff is for my susceptibilities a sure-fire emotional rain-maker. I am not of the generation fortunate enough to have seen George M. Cohan at his vaudeville zenith, but once at an Actors' Fund benefit I heard him twang out "Give My Regards to Broadway" and saw him momentarily break into his old soft-shoe routine and I wept as copiously as an Irishman listening to "Mother Machree" through a fair amount of Scotch mist.

And I recall another occasion some fifteen or more years ago when I gave vent to lachrymose longing for those golden theatrical days that are no more and not that I never remotely shared them. This was when in a tragically futile attempt to revive old-time vaudeville (and a sad commentary on the American public it is that the beloved patient failed to be resuscitated) some enterprising management persuaded the team of Weber and Fields, with the vocal assistance of Fay Templeton, to come forth from retirement and play a week at the Palace. The immortal comedians went through their still side-splitting German-American act in fine form and Fay Templeton sang "Lou-Lou, how I love my Lou," weighing well over two hundred but still looking dainty, dimpled and darling, and I, beholding them all in the flesh for the first time in my life, but determinedly steeped in tradition, melted into such emotional mush one might have taken me for a moony relict of the original Floradora sextette.

I guess I enjoy crying. And this is no purging confession. I don't apologize for a single nose-wipe. If the art of the theatre—or even the "schmaltz" of the theatre (and who is to say that good "schmaltz" is *not* art?) can give us such honest and humanizing means of release may we not welcome them amid the exigencies of a world grown too terrible for tears?

The Sea-Tossed Muse

The Sea-Tossed Muse

WE all have our little illusions about our own mental abilities. An ever recurring illusion of mine . . . recurring, that is, any time I take an ocean voyage, is that I am capable of intellectual concentration on board a ship. Why years of setting out with suitcases loaded beyond their Plimsoll mark with books which never get unpacked shouldn't have taught me that at sea my mind goes blank, I don't know. Yet that recently I booked passage on a slow vessel during an off-travel season for the express purpose of accomplishing a special writing job may well be an indication that my mind must be in a chronic state, far worse than blank.

Whoever has attempted a writing stint on an ocean liner has in all likelihood gone through similar frustrations. The first morning out, you rise a-tingle with salt air and splendid resolutions and after breakfast go armed with work paraphernalia up onto the promenade deck. It's a fine day and you feel that perhaps a brisk turn in the fresh air will clear the brain and start the ideas going. Besides, on shipboard in the morning there are always a few important things to see about . . . such as whether the ocean is still there and if so what condition it's in and whether or not there's anything interesting on it such as another ship or a whale or that seaweed at sight of which seasoned travelers look knowing and say "Gulf Stream." Then it's always a good thing to find out in which direction the wind is blowing. A blast of soot direct from the stack into the eye answers that and after gouging it out, along with several eyelashes and a hunk of lower lid, you decide you've had enough ozone and start looking around for a nice quiet place in which to work.

At first it seems that your own deck chair would be just the ticket. You have chosen one off by itself in a location away from the deck-chair line. To be sure it's right next to a locker from which the sailor in charge of games periodically extracts ping-pong and shuffleboard equipment each time that he does so saying pardon him Madam and you replying that it's quite all right. But that is a minor drawback. You stretch out comfortably, a steward comes up and straitjackets your feet and legs in a blanket. You heave a happy and resolute "*Now*, then!" open pad, poise pencil and start to work.

That is, you start to start. Whoever has gone through the excruciating preliminaries to a writing job will know whereof I speak. It's a case of anything to lead up to writing, meaning anything to postpone the horrid moment of having to begin. There are all sorts of ruses that come in handy. First of all there are those pencils that have to be sharpened and if you're on the deck of a ship, the sharpener won't be the reliable desk variety, but one of those nasty little pocket gadgets which shatters the wood into fine kindling and affects the lead in such a way that it falls out in pieces the moment it touches paper. But that's all right because this serves as an excuse for the further delay of re-sharpening.

Other methods of writing postponement are the plotting of that outline you think you're going to follow . . . an early conditioning dating back to the days when you "took" Emerson and Thoreau and wrote themes with titles like "A Spring Walk with my Dog" which teacher drummed into you must have an exposition, a development and a conclusion. Then there's the sorting over of those notes so vitally relative to the topic you're going to write about. They make for fascinating reading especially when you come across some notes on another and, at this point, far more interesting topic along with a letter which ought really to be answered and the address, which ought really to be entered in your book, of those nice people who said if you ever came to Denmark to be sure to look them up.

There comes the moment when you can't find any more excuses for postponement and you begin, more nilly than willy, the painful, plodding placing of one word after the other known as writing.

It may be that at first all goes well. The opening sentence and even a few ensuing ones may actually seem to write themselves. Then the distractions start . . . beginning with those early morning oh-be-joyfuls who greet each other with clarion "good-MORNings" and "how are-YOU-todays" followed by a lot of antiphonal "just-fines." Then start the deck-walkers, some of whom you begin to wish were plank-walkers . . . especially as every time they go by, some idiotic compulsion makes you look up at them. The fat ladies who toddle, the small children who skip . . . and also squeal, the distinguished foreigners in berets who stroll distinguishedly, gloved hands clasped behind their back, the professorial types whose pipes are always having to be cleaned and dumped amid loud tapping noises. And most irritating of all, some of those clear-eyed hiking couples who, lacking the Matterhorn, settle on the deck to conquer by striding around it fifty times. As they make their rounds with increasingly purposeful vigor, you begin to wish for a torch to hand them saying "Marathon's just out and beyond that railing, friends."

You determine not to be so weakmindedly distracted by this inconsequential passing parade and resolutely lower your eyes to the work at hand. But there comes a moment when the parade doesn't pass. Instead a number form an eager little cluster by the railing, someone points to something out on the sea which their massed presence hides from view and the rest come out with tantalizing remarks such as "Oh *look!*" or "Yes, I *do* see it!" or "How can you tell that's what it is?" until you're driven to go see for yourself and by the time you've emerged from your blanket cocoon and have arrived at the railside, the spectators have dispersed and whatever *it* was has vanished into the briny. You return to your chair and, the steward being nowhere around, try awkwardly to re-wrap your own lower extremities in a puffing contortionist act during which you drop first the pad, which flutters in the wind, then the pencil, which rolls out of reach, then your bag which falls open and upside down . . . while a dead-pan pair in nearby chairs watch with steady intensity.

Finally, you collect your scattered effects and a few of your equally scattered thoughts and manage to write some more words. The morning promenade has let up, quiet prevails and you begin to realize the amenities of a slow ship. The idyll is shattered by the arrival of what always strikes me as the least amenity of any ship, slow or rapid, morning bouillon. What sea-faring tradition ever gave rise to this soggy snack is as incomprehensible as why the docile passenger who downs it doesn't almost immediately give rise to *it*.

Eventually it becomes clear that the deck chair is not a locale conducive to writing. As a matter of personal opinion, I find the deck chair, after a period of time, not conducive to much beyond acute discomfort. The semi-recumbent, semi-prenatal position one is forced statically to maintain has a hemlock-drinking effect on the anatomy. First the feet go numb, then the knees, followed shortly by the thighs and by the time my fanny goes to sleep, unlike Socrates, I decide it's time to get up and go below to the privacy of my cabin.

Whoever has attempted to do any writing in a ship's cabin knows the drawbacks of this sanctuary, even if one of them isn't the presence of the steward and stewardess who are still in the process of fixing it up. The paramount question is what to use for a desk. The dressing table is an obvious choice, but there's no space for the knees and to sit for an hour or so in the twisted position of a side-saddle rider grows painful. Moreover there is a lot of surface interference in the way of jars that must be moved, bottles that topple over, a powder box that spills and one long horrid human hair which keeps turning up across the page. The alternate choice is to move to the armchair, an uncompromising little number as heavy as lead and as low as a kindergarten stool, and write either on the lap or the edge of the bed bent double in a Quasimodo position in which, if you're susceptible to muscular spasm, you're likely to be cast for the remainder of the day. Because in all probability, you'll be plunk in the middle of a draft . . . either from one of those wind-tunnel ventilators which you have to keep getting up to adjust, or from the porthole which, because early that morning the sun was out, you summoned the steward to open but which, now that the sun has retired behind inky clouds and there looks to be a typhoon brewing, you resummon him to close. The exclusion of all drafts means the exclusion of all air and you open the outer door, forgetting, of course, to hook it. It bangs to and fro in happy rhythm with the movement of the ship until you rise in wrath and addressing it by a term permissible only in Shakespearean historical drama, fasten it to the wall and return to your work, by which time the door in the adjacent cabin starts banging. The sight of an open cabin door is an overwhelming temptation for passers-by to pause and look in. And when they do, you pause to look up and this makes for little moments of pretty confusion.

Amid all those frustrations, I have failed to mention the greatest impediment to mental activity on board a ship, namely the persistent battle against sleep. During those first drugged days at sea you struggle valiantly against the temptation to take just a little catnap . . . which, in your doped state, would end up a sleep less cat than swine. It's only the fear of your mouth falling open that prevents you from snoozing off in a deck chair, whereas in your cabin the fear is that if you give in, you'll never again wake up.

During my own recent venture, I abandoned the deck chair and cabin as locales for creative work and went in search of more propitious surroundings. That annoying sense that one should make the most of the sea air which is not only fresh but also free, prompted me at first to look for a place out in the open. But most of the open areas were far too much so and more a setting for the memoirs of Joan Lowell provided she were equipped with wind-resistant paper and a pen that writes under salt spray. Eventually I found a secluded bench on the top deck, snugly sheltered from the wind. It was also in the direct line of a strong smell of frying from the kitchen ventilator, but that merely added to its coziness. It became less cozy with the sudden bounding entrance of a foursome of British hearties, all blazers, white shoes and fearful enthusiasm and out to preserve the Empire with a ripping good game of deck tennis. My secluded bench served obviously as a bleacher stand and this was the beginning of a tournament. Meekly I gave way to the deck tennis fans and sought further seclusion.

This time it was to a region which the show-off voyager chooses to call "below aft," namely down and out toward the stern in an open space used, while at dock, for lowering things like automobiles into the hold. Now it was used as a recreational area for soiled personages from the engine room out to enjoy a few minutes of leisure. This trip it was used also as a lodging area for two horses stalled up for eight days of enforced leisure. Whether or not they were enjoying theirs is debatable, but they furnished a good deal of enjoyment for certain sight-seeing-minded passengers who came down periodically to feed them sugar and gaze at them with an interest worthy the duck-billed platypus. I too seemed to serve as an object of minor zoological interest, for as they passed me perched as I was on the hatch with feet braced against an iron crossbar, they would hesitate as though to offer me too a lump of sugar, while certain of the more chummy types, after watching what I was doing for a bit would enquire brightly "writing?"

Even without the horse visitors, there were distractions, chief of which being my own stream of consciousness, occasioned by the least significant incident. I had, for example, to shake myself out of an agreeable ten-minute reverie brought on by the sight of an American girl over behind a funnel who was carrying on a lovely flirtation with a junior officer . . . a pretty picture which started me wondering nostalgically what ever happened to that handsome radio operator years ago on the *Vulcania*, the one who looked the way an Italian tenor ought to and who, although gifted with no ray of intellect, nevertheless had an intoxicating way of kissing not only the back of the hand but the inside of the forearm and who . . . Oh to hell with that radio operator and back to work, my gal!

Further interruption came when a very young, very pink-cheeked assistant steward happened by, and, because I must have looked lonely out there on the hatch, felt obliged to engage me in conversation to which I, because he reminded me of my son whom he in no way resembled, felt obliged to reply. We discussed the weather, the rolling talents of the ship, if we were likely to pass close to the *Queen Mary* and whether I'd ever had the privilege of meeting Marilyn Monroe. I tried to terminate each fascinating exchange of ideas with a periodic "Well, then" indicative of dismissal, but the youth remained as firmly planted as a guardsman and it was I who did my own uprooting.

Reluctantly I went inside, trying first a room labeled "Library," a quiet retreat equipped with polite little writing desks and a polite little collection of books running the literary gamut from E. Phillips Oppenheim to *The Robe*. All the desks were occupied by people using up the free stationery. The only place was at one of those vis-à-vis tables at where two people sit facing each other over a letter rack, nervously avoiding each other's glances. My opposing partner was a little old lady from the Midlands . . . one of those professional quainties who spread incessant cheer in a determinedly North Country accent. Although it was only the third day out, she was busying herself with customs declaration, chirping to some near-by cronies how they'd best get busy and fill out their wee slips. After I moved out of the library and onto the comparative quiet of an in-door verandah, she appeared again and started explaining to a complete stranger how she'd best manage the wee stitches of her wee crocheting. She kept turning up, a Nemesis of interruption, clear across the ocean . . . on deck, in the lounge, even in my own cabin when, one rough day at a sudden roll of the ship she hurtled with a little squeal across the threshold and I barely restrained myself from cautioning her that she'd best be careful or she'd fall and break her wee damn neck.

Next morning, I hit on the idea of trying the big formal room known as the main Saloon. A curious appellation as nothing stronger than tea was ever served in it and nothing more sinister than Bingo took place in it. To be sure, certain afternoons it was the scene of some merry two shilling betting on the progress of small wooden sticks down a baize carpet, known as horse-racing, and alternate evenings to the Bingo galas, it presented, under the heading of Cinema, grade B pictures of the early 1940's. But mornings, at least, it was quiet. I found a table and pulled over a chair . . . or rather, the chair pulled me over, for not only cast iron in weight, it was anchored to the floor. I settled on a gilt chair from the band stand, spread out my papers and set to work. Conditions seemed ideal. The place was deserted as a tomb.

That is, until 10:45 . . . at which time the tomb became as populated as the Capulet family vault in the last scene of Romeo and Juliet. The mid-morning concert, a divertissement furnished by the ship's dance band, was about to begin and the music lovers were assembling in happy anticipation. They were headed by (need I say) the dear little character from the

North Country who informed us all that it was she who had chosen the opening selection . . . a bonnie number known as "The Wee MacGregor."

I beat a hasty retreat to the enclosed verandah where MacGregor come booming out over the PA system, amplified to proportions anything but wee.

I finally solved the situation to a certain degree. In the quiet little forward bar was a quiet little backward writing desk. Here silence prevailed all morning, the only sound being toward noon, the soothing plopping of olives and cherries into cocktail glasses by the discreet bartender. At the twelve o'clock whistle the ship's sporting contingent gathered to see who'd won the pool on the day's run, by which time I myself was quite ready anyway to knock off work and if the winner were the expansive sort, to accept modestly any proffered drink. Afternoons, the same peace and quiet prevailed and thanks to the bar I was able to finish off my job. I came close to finishing off my reputation as well. After landing, as I stood by my bags in the customs shed I overheard a woman saying to a friend who had come to meet her "See that person over there?" and she inclined her head in my direction. "She's an alcoholic. My dear, she spent each and every entire day in the bar! Isn't that awful?"

Next time I take a trip I'll tag my mind "Not Wanted on the Voyage" and enter into shipboard life. Who knows? I might even become addicted to Bingo and morning bouillon!

Biblio-Technique

Biblio-Technique

BEING a Francophile, I hesitate ever to make the all too prevalent comment of Americans who when confronted with certain involved Gallic methods and customs come out with a righteous "We do this better at home." I prefer the more moderate view that we do it differently. For instance, I'd never dream of suggesting that our way of running a public library is better than that of the French, but I can honestly proclaim that the technique of obtaining reading matter in Paris' *Bibliothèque Nationale* differs as widely from that of New York's Public Library as *escargots* from cheeseburgers.

I recently had occasion to do some research in this world's greatest book repository. It was a bright, sunny day when I set forth on my initial visit. Little Parisian clouds were dancing across a gay blue sky and over

the Rivoli arches of the Louvre, a tricolor wigwagged
to remind all pedestrians that they were treading the
most delectable pavements of Europe. With eager ela-
tion I hastened along the rue de Richelieu. The massive
grey wall of the great library loomed into sight making
me feel awed and purposeful. French respect for schol-
arship manifested by a street-sign saying "SILENCE!
BIBLIOTHEQUE!" added to my awe and I found
myself walking on tiptoe and about to say hush to a
passing bus. A main entrance led into a spacious courtyard flanked by 17th Century buildings that looked
to be former palaces . . . whose, I don't know, although in that section of the city it's always safe to
say Mazarin. An arrow pointed to a public entry across
the court and a severe no-smoking sign warned that
it was:

DEFENSE ABSOLUTE
TO FUME
UNDER PAIN OF
IMMEDIATE EXCLÚSION.

The chill of this reception was mitigated by a warm
welcome from the Bibliothèque cat, a weedy little
tabby who, in lieu of the invariable carved lion who
guards the portals of American libraries, keeps morning
watch at the foot of the entrance steps, arching her
back for whoever will pause to stroke it. At noon she
knocks off for déjeuner along with the rest of Paris,
and afternoons she follows the sun to doze on the roof
slates.

After paying respects to the cat, I went up the

steps and into a marble foyer. The words SALLE DE LECTURE emblazoned over a doorway indicated that I was directly in front of the reading-room. "This is a cinch" I thought and walked confidently in through the door. However, not very far in, for I was stopped by a voice . . . unquestionably one of authority as it issued from a man wearing that indefinable semi-uniform which denotes the public functionary. He sat at a table on which a telephone gave the sinister impression of being in direct communication with the prefect of police.

"Your permit, Madame," he said.

"My permit?" I echoed. But yes, he repeated, one must exhibit one's permit. "A permit for what?" I croaked. But obviously, he said, a permit to get out books. He made it sound like a permit to carry concealed weapons. Reacting as I do when up against French officialdom, I said Oh meekly and looked helpless. France being the last outpost of gallantry, the sight of a female in distress melts the heart of the most red-tape-bound official. In softened tones he told me that if I would address myself to the *bureau* which found itself out in the foyer, one would occupy one's self of me. I thanked him and went to get myself occupied of. A door marked BUREAU led into a small passageway, dark, airless and jammed with a line-up of permit applicants. Through a glass partition one could see into the inner office where a man was leaning over a counter talking earnestly to a lady seated on the other side. She was making long and serious notations in a ledger. After considerable time, he emerged and the next in line entered the star chamber to go through similar secret procedure. The queue advanced at snail's pace. Meanwhile, we all eyed one another in the hostile manner of patients in the waiting-room of a throat specialist.

At long last my turn arrived and I found myself confronting the lady in the inner sanctum. Without looking up from her ledger she said good day, Madame, and what was it about, Madame. Madame said it was about a permit. Did I wish to obtain a permit, she asked, and I answered with the French equivalent of yes if it was all right by her. She gave me a blank to fill out and at the same time asked what I wanted the permit for. "To read," I said. "To read what?" she said, and I said "Books." She wrote down *imprimés* which I had always thought meant *printed matter* but when I added "Also newspapers," she wrote down *journaux* too,—newspapers, it would seem, being still in a state of hand illumination. For some reason she seemed to be taking a slightly contemptuous view of me, so much so that, when she asked me my profession, I came out rather grandly with "Actress," hoping to impress her. She gave me a quick, appraising look, then returned to her ledger. Obviously the only impression made upon her was that I was lying. She then stunned me by asking the name of the university from which I had received my degree. Actually I have never in my life received any legitimate degree although over the years certain colleges have generously bestowed on me

some totally undeserved honorary ones. I thought specifically of Mills, Tufts and Temple. "Meels" I told
her proudly "Et aussi Toofts, *et* l'Université du Temple." This created the impression that mention of my
profession had failed to produce. In tones of respect
she asked for identification papers and I handed her my
passport. Her respect was short-lived. "But this is not
you!" she exclaimed. At first I thought she referred to
my picture and felt rather flattered until I saw she
was pointing to my name, which on the passport was
my married one. . . . I had used my professional name
on the blank. I tried to explain the discrepancy but
she cut me off by handing me an entirely fresh blank
to fill out while, quite irritably, she made erasures in
her ledger. I felt a bit sheepish seeing her write "Mme.
Blodget, artiste de théâtre."

All this was taking up time. I glanced nervously
through the glass partition at the waiting line-up. Their
expressions denoted the "Aaah!" and "Voyons, voyons!" of Gallic exasperation. Eventually the lady
handed me my permit, not before making some cabalistic notations in her ledger. After the passport incident, I felt that they must be of an incriminating nature.

Muttering a series of "Pardonnez-moi"s I scurried
out through the passageway and into the Salle de
Lecture where I handed the permit to the uniformed
guard. He read everything written on it, as if seeing
such a thing for the first time, nodded pontifical approval and handed me a cardboard shingle on which
was stamped the number 238. There's no selecting

one's own seat in the Bibliothèque. No. 238 was my allotted place and there I must sit even if the man on my right reeked of garlic and the lady on my left had a bad cold and coughed like an atomizer in my direction.

The Salle de Lecture is a gem of Second Empire incongruity. All glass domes, gilded iron pillars and allegorical murals, its designer must have tried to combine the glories of the Crystal Palace, Versailles and the Albert Memorial. Presiding over the room, on a raised platform, is the *Contrôle*, three impressive individuals who sit church-elder fashion behind a golden oak structure that bears a distressing resemblance to a police desk. A man in the center is flanked on either side by a stalwart woman . . . one of those indomitable matriarchs, those "real men of France" wearing, instead of trousers, the inevitable black dustcoat of the Parisian working woman. These are the oligarchs who take and file away all permits and seat numbers before readers embark upon the perilous venture of looking up their books.

This rite takes place down on a lower floor in a room marked CATALOGUES BIBLIOGRAPHIES which, as I was informed that first day, finds itself in descending the stairs to the left. The room may find itself but it was days before I found myself wise to its workings. On my initial visit, these were not immediately apparent, for at the foot of the stairs, rows of weighty volumes, handsomely bound and marked "authors," made things look to be as easy as pumpkin pie.

The pie, however, soon turned into mince. Of the books on my reading list, one was by Jacques Wilhelm and the other by the writer, Willy, and there was no volume for authors whose names began with W. At a nearby desk, a kindly-looking man with the flowing moustache of an early Gaul seemed to be vaguely in charge. I told him of my predicament. Ah no, he explained ruefully, the handsomely bound books extended only through the letter M. So what did one do, I asked. But obviously, he said, one looked them up in the next room in the volumes less handsomely bound, a condition he appeared to deplore. I made a think-nothing-of-it gesture and went in search of the *W* authors. Willy I found, but there was no trace of the works of Wilhelm. I returned with the news to the kindly Gaul. Ah but, he said, still ruefully, what was the publication date of the desired book? I had no more idea of its date than I had of that of his birthday. Obviously, Madame, he went on all books published since 1935 are listed on catalogue cards in the index filing cabinets *là-bas* either on the right or on the left. I said Oh and went *là-bas* in search of Monsieur Wilhelm whom it took a bare fifteen minutes to find.

Tracking down author and title is only the beginning of the game. Next came the fun of filling out the request slips. These, some green, some grey, were stacked on handy writing counters. I selected a green one and sat down to study it. A perforation down the middle divides two halves on both of which a great deal has to be written. On the left is something called a "souche" which it says is to be left in the stacks . . . by whom it doesn't say. On this must be written one's name and address, one's seat number, the date, the listing of the desired literary work, the date of its publication (the French are nuts for dates) and something called a *tomaison* which has to do with number of volumes. On the right of the perforation, all the above information must be repeated, plus the name of author, title of book, the place of publication with, of course, *its* date and a *format* which, it warns, "must also figure below in the stack listing when, in the catalogue, it precedes the letter of the series." The meaning of this last injunction, I decided to figure out in my own good time. What immediately stymied me was that item about my seat number. I knew where it was, I hadn't thought to memorize it. This meant that I had to slink back upstairs to the *Contrôle*, confess my delinquency to the matriarch who had filed my place number and stand on one unhappy foot after the other while she went over the files of everyone who had come in that morning. Finally she came across mine and told me my number was 238 in tones so loud a few nearby readers glared and emitted those hissing sounds which are French for "Shut up!"

Feeling somewhat cowed, I returned to the CATA-LOGUES and the business of filling out the request slip. The next problem was that blank space beside *format*. I knew that the French word *format* in English is *format*, the one rhyming with *Norma*, the other with *doormat*, but that didn't make me know what to put down. I went back to the desk and consulted the kindly Gaul. "Monsieur," I began "Je suis bien stupide . . ." He smiled charmingly and gave a non-committal shrug which could have meant "Madame exaggerates" or "Madame doesn't express the half of it." The *format*, he explained with the patience of a teacher of backward children, indicated the appearance of the book in question. My impulse was to ask how the hell you'd know until you saw it, but instead I said Oh. Further explanation informed me I must copy off from the filing card a cabalistic little 4° or 8° printed in numerals so small, it required strong light and my glasses held at a much increased magnifying angle to decipher. I returned to the counter and, to make certain, copied off everything except an inkstain. In addition to author, title, my name, address and the current date there was (and all repeated twice)

Paris 10, faub., Montmartre (1915)
In. . . .fol, 160 p. fig.,
portr., planche en coul., carte
Fol $1h^4$ 2737

Proud as if I'd solved a chemistry problem, I took the result up to the scholarly Gaul, certain he'd give me an A. He gave me instead a sorrowful look. "But you've done it in pencil, Madame!" he said. I said Oh and returned to the writing counter. Not having a pen with me, I was obliged to use the one placed there for public use. It was barnacled with generations of ink and the nib was splayed like an olive fork, but I managed to make out a new slip which, with a trium-

phant "Voilà!" I submitted for the inspection of my
Early Gaul. I almost burst into sobs when again he
shook a rueful head. Though still patient it was clear
he had never before had to deal with such mental
delinquency. "But Madame! Your seat number is 238,
yes?" I agreed that it sure yes was. The experience of
retrieving it had ingrained itself upon what remained
of my mind. "But you have made this out on a green
slip!" He was as incredulous as though I'd made it
out on a laundry slip. I then learned that the occupants
of seats numbering from 1 through 181 use green slips,
all others use grey. I returned to the counter and made
out a grey one. Practice gave me confidence, and I
went so far as to make out a second one for a second
book.

Request slips are deposited at the *Contrôle* desk in
a sort of square can into whose maw, amid grinding
noises like a garbage disposer, they disappear and apparently journey down into the subterranean laby-
rinths of Paris. There certain Jean Valjeans search out
the requested volumes, send them by unseen means up
to smock-clad attendants who make periodic deliveries
to the readers. There is a rumor that the Bibliothèque
contains some seven kilometers of books . . . which
is not hard to believe. And it's not hard to believe
either that the Jean Valjeans walk the full seven before
they send up your book. Meanwhile you sit at your
place and wait. There is something about this interim
which is disturbingly like waiting in an exam room for

the passing of College Board papers. My seat was directly before the *Contrôle* whose members took on the aspect of proctors. I was afraid to glance at what the persons on either side were reading for fear I'd be called up for cheating. The wait seemed interminable. I regretted not having brought a magazine with me or some postcards of the Eiffel Tower to send home. Even some knitting would have come in handy.

At last an attendant came along with our section's allotment of books. He set down one of mine, then reproachfully handed me back my request slip for the other, telling me I had, in one place, neglected to write in today's date. "Couldn't someone have written it in?" I asked in a whisper. He answered in anything but a whisper that it must be in the applicant's writing. I said Oh and wrote 6/28/53. By the time *that* book appeared, I had been in the Bibliothèque exactly two hours.

After this first initiation, things went more easily. I learned to make out request slips with speed and accuracy even when the catalogue cards were not printed but handwritten and with those curious French numerals which look like ancient musical notes. A few minor complications kept routine from becoming humdrum. One was when through some mysterious mix-up my permit got exchanged with someone else's. It was pretty confusing to discover that I was going about under the guise of "Mlle. Dominique Vincent, étudiante" but nothing comparable to the confusion which must have been that of Mlle. Vincent when she found herself identified as "Mme. Blodget, artiste de théâtre."

Then there was the day when in all innocence I applied for a volume of short articles by certain humorous journalists which, it later developed, were of a fairly scatological nature. Little did I know as I wrote out the catalogue number which was preceded by the letters "RES" that this referred to a Reserve Room, entry to which is gained only by special permission. It never occurred to me that the French would take the same sort of austere measures as those observed in Boston's respectable Athenaeum where volumes frowned upon by the Watch and Ward Society are segregated in a discreet sanctuary known as "The Scruple Room." It was quite harassing therefore to find myself called up before the *Contrôle* and asked by one of the official matriarchs my purpose in wanting this particular book. Feeling as guilty as if I'd been caught trying to sneak out a copy of "The Memoirs of Fanny Hill," I explained that it dealt with the period I was studying. But, she said, I must apply for a permit from the Monsieur at the center desk who at the moment was out for lunch. I hardly felt that the book was worth a two-hour wait.

Another time when I tried for a permit, it proved to be the Monsieur's day off. Let me reassure the pure in mind that the mysteries of France's Scruple Room to me remain as unknown as the forbidden frescoes of Pompeii.

I did brave the Periodical Room. Not, however, without the assistance of a helpful young Frenchman, a research specialist who volunteered to put me wise to its intricacies. In order to save time, he went to look up the newspapers I wanted to see while I sat and familiarized myself with the rules and regulations of this department. These were printed on a leaflet handed out by an official at the door and they went like this (I quote at random):

"Reproduce the indication of the fascicle in one of the compartments which find themselves in the "recto" of the present leaflet. Return the bulletin to one of the guards of the periphery, before the Roman numeral of the number of the Catalogue . . ."

I gave up and sat idly waiting for the return of the nice Frenchman. It was some fifteen minutes before he reappeared and minus the periodicals. They were, it seemed, not in the Periodical but back in the regular reading room. He looked as harassed as I usually did and my most solacing moment was when with a profound sigh he said "C'est bien compliqué!" My proudest moment was one day when a bewildered Frenchwoman asked *me* how to make out her slip! And my most endearing was after my final visit as I went out across the sunny courtyard: the sight of the kindly Gaul of the CATALOGUES BIBLIOGRAPHIES, solemnly undoing the paper wrapping of his meagre lunch and sharing a generous chunk of his *jambon* sandwich with the little Bibliothèque cat.

That Which We
Call a Street

That Which We
Call a Street

BOULEVARD
POISSONNIERE
BOULEVARD
BONNE NOUVELLE
BOULEVARD
Sᵀ DENIS
BOULEVARD
Sᵀ MARTIN
PLACE
DE LA REPUBLIQUE

TO THOSE who know Paris well, the fact that her tortuous streets keep changing their names every few blocks is no more surprising than that the Seine follows an equally tortuous course, shifting the geographic locale of its two banks so that, at certain points, the Right Bank is east of the left, at others, north of it and, along about Passy, it turns up in the region of the setting sun. Baffling to the uninitiated as may be the changing course of Paris' river, the changing nomenclature of her streets is even more baffling . . . especially to the American tourist when feeling the atmospheric thing to do is to go for one of those "boulevard strolls" he's heard so much about. Trustingly he sets out along the Boulevard de la Madeleine and in no time at all, instead of the street of that sanctified sinner, he discovers he is strolling down that of the Capucines (which he can take as either nasturtiums or lady Capuchin monks according to his fancy). Just a block or so further, the Capucines give way to the Italiens and these outlanders shortly cede precedence to Montmartre which with an Alice-in-Wonderland-like trick is transformed into a Fishwife as our bewildered pedestrian finds himself treading the noisy pavements of the Boulevard Poissonnière. However, not for long . . . for all at once he is sprinting down a stretch which goes by the cheerful name of Bonne Nouvelle (what *was* this good news that a whole district should rejoice in its name?) but then, lest he become frivolously over-elated, two saints produce their sobering effect as the boulevard comes into the possession first of St. Denis, then of St. Martin and finally, as if at a loss for any more names, terminates in the Place de la République.

However, if our traveler wishes to continue his role of ambulatory *boulevardier* and, provided his feet are still intact, he can jog to the right across this Place which honors the Républic and continue, still on a boulevard which starts out as that of the Temple and after crossing the Place Pasdeloup (named, I suppose after the conductor responsible for the Pasdeloup concerts . . . although more amusing is the literal translation of "wolf-step" or could it be "wolf-trot"?) the boulevard turns pious under the influence of the Filles de Calvaire. But these daughters of Calvary exert their piety for only a short distance as the highway continues under the gay aegis of that author of gay drama, Beaumarchais, until it runs wham against the column of the Place de la Bastille. But this need not end our hero's stroll, for branching out from this heroic site of arson and bloodshed are three more boulevards of which he can take his pick according to his mood. If it is a French Revolutionary one, he may continue on down the Boulevard de la Bastille. If it is one of picaresque gallantry, the Boulevard Henri IV may prove more to his taste, while his third alternative is a Boulevard Bourdon, and not being up on Paris history, I wouldn't know whether this refers to some worthy named Bourdon or to what the word means in English, namely, bumblebee. Whichever his choice, this will turn out to be the last leg of his jaunt for each of these three boulevards, without a single shift of name, ends abruptly in a Quai of the river Seine, in whose waters he may seek oblivion if crazed by blistered feet and the cockeyed realization that for hours he has been walking steadily along an undeviating thoroughfare which, since he embarked upon it, has gone by twelve different names.

I should like to get by with pretending to be enough of a Paris habituée to have followed from memory the peregrinations of our wanderer down this highway of many titles. But I must confess to having done some flagrant cheating, my "trot" being that handy little red booklet for sale at every *librairie* and newspaper kiosk, containing not only a large plan of Paris, but individual maps of each *arrondissement* and aptly known as "The Indispensable." No wise tourist sets forth without it and even a Frenchman shows no shame in consulting its invaluable pages when confronted with some transportational problem such as how to go by Metro from, say, the rue des Sablons to the rue de Montsouris . . . in other words from the Street of the Fine Sands to the Street of Mouse Mountain. The names started me pouring over this fascinating tiny volume with its lists of streets, bridges, squares, "cités," passages and even impasses. For a spare hour, I can recommend no more diverting pursuit. It is one of those forms of intellectual peanut-eating like looking up something in the encyclopaedia and being unable to stop because of all the attendant distractions. One is first arrested by those image-provoking byways of the Left Bank . . . the Fishing Cat, the Four Winds, the Old Dove-Cote, the Two Angels and that touching little street called "Gît-le-Coeur" indicating the tender fact that there lies a heart, one hopes in peace. It seems atmospherically fitting that the Left Bank should harbor a street to St. Anthony-of-the-Arts as well as all those which suggest the small trades . . . the Street of the Scissors, of the Wooden Shoe, the Passage of the Little Butcher-Shop, the Street of He who Grinds Rose Madder (a possibly over-free translation of the rue Garancière). There is also a Madam Street, but whether or not this has any bearing on a well-known trade, one doesn't know. Less ambiguous seems that street which is ever in search of the noon-hour, the Cherche-Midi, an appetite-provoking title which rings in the imagination like a luncheon-bell.

Across the river in and about the Saint Antoine district, once associated with knitting women and the Revolution, more recently with certain small restaurants whose specialities are derived from produce less of the regular market than of the black, there, appropriately enough, are to be found the Street of the Bad Boys, of the Golden Hand, the Three Faces (an impasse), The Four Thieves and one which goes by the conjectural name of the Street of the Minimum. Further west, in the financial district of the Bourse, it's rather pleasing to find a Pick-Pocket Street while in the expensive regions of St. Honoré where the guileless haunt the catch-tourist shops, the Street of the Innocents ends extravagantly enough in Lingerie Street.

Up around the Arc de Triomphe it is no more surprising that thoroughfares should bear witness to France's victories and military heroes than that in the affluent residential districts branching out from this monument to "la Gloire," the blue and white corner signs should immortalize monarchs and foreign dignitaries. Here we find Francois 1ᵉʳ, George V, Peter the First of Serbia, President Wilson and Alfonso the 13th. Here also are streets dedicated to Byron and Chateaubriand, but lest to the high-born this appear to be an over-bohemian intrusion, let them recall the reassuring fact that the poet was an English Lord and the novelist a French Viscount.

You can really get carried away by perusal of this comprehensive little booklet and, if you're in a semischolarly frame of mind and arm yourself with an encyclopaedia, or better still, the biographical section of that most compact of reference books, the "Petit Larousse," you end up by giving yourself an entire home-study course in French history, beginning with the Roman Conquest and finishing with the Liberation as the rue Jules César and the Avenue Franklin Delano Roosevelt flank the span of two thousand years. Between them lies an intricate network commemorative of the glittering past and comprehensively catholic enough to satisfy members of every faction from diehard royalist to kill-hard radical. That elegantly fantastic character who calls himself "the last of the Bonapartists" and haunts the book stalls of the Quais dressed like the duc de Morny must derive haughty satisfaction from the number of avenues, streets and squares which sing of Napoleon and his victories. The gory glories of the Revolution are immortalized and with a true Gallic impartiality which could arouse no complaints from Monarchist, Jacobin or Girondist, for we find a rue Lamballe named for the princess whose head fell by order of Danton, who himself has a street as has, in turn the man who caused *his* head to roll, Robespierre, while the advocate Malesherbes who defended Louis XVI has an entire boulevard and one that doesn't even once change its title.

The patriotically minded (and who in France isn't?) must rejoice in the rue de la Marseillaise and the fact that the rues Liberté, Egalité and Fraternité all run into each other, while even the most left of leftists can't feel that his cause is neglected for, in addition to an avenue named after his socialist hero Jean Juarez, there's a Leningrad Street and a Place Stalingrad. But let there be no alarm among the remaining royalists (and a surprising lot of the old dears do remain). They may tap their jewelled snuff-boxes over the countless highways and byways to the greater glory of the Royal Line . . . Valois, Bourbon, Orleáns, Navarre and a variety of kings from the Louis who bore the title of saint to the one who bore the umbrella, Louis-Philippe. Native appreciation of philandering in the grand manner manifests itself in the number of thoroughfares in honor of Henry the Fourth. France's most dashing monarch can boast a boulevard, a passage, a gate, a quai, and a street which merges, romantically and logically with that of La Belle Gabrielle, his mistress. Gabrielle d'Estrees is not the only light-o'-love thus immortalized. Madame de Maintenon has, of all things, an alley. There's a street named de Poitiers which I for one would like to believe is named after Henry 2nd's exquisite Diane (I think I shall anyway). There is also one for Adrienne Lecouvreur, whose talents were equally divided between the boards of the stage and those of the boudoir. It is agreeable to note that the Avenue de Saxe (the name of her most famous lover) is in the same arrondissement while her good friend

Voltaire (who rates a boulevard, a street, a place and a "cité") is cruelly distant on another bank of the Seine. (Imagine if an American street were named after a worldly woman the hue and cry that would arise from all our national leagues of Chronic Indignation!)

Reformers who take offense at such frivolity may derive a certain amount of repent-ye satisfaction from the presence of an Impasse Satan and a Passage of Hell. While the more benevolent clergy can be gently pleased with Ave Maria Square, the Cité Grace-of-God and a serene street identified as "Lands of the Curé." There are, for the benefit of religious zealots, saints galore . . . over a hundred and fifty of them . . . the gentlemen saints ranging from St. Albin to St. Yves, the lady saints from Ste. Anastasia to one going by the practical name of Ste. Opportune. All of these do not, of course, come under the heading of canonization, as in the case of the critic Sainte Beuve (what critic was ever saintly?) or that monster of the Revolution Saint Just (what quirk of French irony would make them name anything after him!). I'm not certain if Saint Emillion refers to a very good man or a very good wine and I wouldn't know about one named Saint Fiacre . . . although the idea of there being a St. Cab seems quite endearing and, in the case of Paris, most appropriate.

After saints, next in profusion come generals . . . forty-four of them (there are eight Captains and of Lieutenants a meagre four) followed by thirty-six doctors. All of which is certainly most admirable. But what strikes one as even more admirable is France's unflagging tribute to literature and the arts. You can't walk a hundred meters without running across a musician, an artist or a writer . . . classic or of recent times. It fills me personally with professional pride to note that the theatre has not been overlooked in the way not only of playwrights but actors as well. Rachel has an avenue, Talma and Mounet Sully have streets and to Réjane and Sarah Bernhardt each a square. Happily too, the best of music hall has been recognized as the memory of Aristide Bruant, the swashbuckling singer of the huge felt hat and flowing red muffler lives on in a street of his beloved Montmartre.

The list is not limited to those who have contributed to the distinction only of France, for generously sprinkled about this civilized capitol are testimonials to the great of other nations. There is Dante Street, Milton Street, Gabriel d'Annunzio Street, Velásquez Avenue and Charles Dickens Square. A two-thousand-year-old hatred has not affected appreciation of Germany's culture, for Beethoven, Goethe and Mendelssohn can each boast a street as can Heinrich Heine even if his first name appears charmingly as Henri. A similar gallicization has occurred in the case of Switzerland's hero who, due to the ever-startling French for William, is listed under the G's as Guillaume Tell, while Tolstoy appears in the fascinating guise of *Lew* Tolstoi! Even barbaric America receives its share of recognition. Beside such national figures as Washington, Franklin and Lincoln, there is a street which honors

Edgar Poe (pronounced Ed-Garr Po-Way) also a couple named Myron C. Herrik and the rue Rockfeller, and spelled exactly that way.

What a colorful and sensible means of paying tribute and how much more felicitous to be memorialized in a thoroughfare which serves as both convenience and constant reminder for passers-by, rather than in an obscure and possibly hideous statue which serves chiefly as a convenience for pigeons!

How pleasant if New York were to go in for similar salute to its heritage, beyond such textbook examples as Columbus Circle, Pershing and Washington Squares and the Hendrick Hudson Parkway. Our writers, artists and musicians go unsung, or rather unvehicularized and even up by the home of the author of "The Raven" (revered as I just pointed out, in Paris) the only recognition comes from the proprietor of an eatery who, more imaginative than our city fathers, keeps bright the bard's name with a sign reading "Poe's Cozy Nook." In our congested island city, if not entire streets, even blocks would serve to keep us more heritage minded. Why isn't some block near the Metropolitan Museum called Winslow Homer and, in the same vicinity, what more elegant address than one on John Singer Sargent Street? Certainly that stretch of 56th onto which Carnegie Hall backs should, in dedication to the beloved conductor who passed so often through its stage door, be called Walter Damrosch Area and what additional anticipatory emotion would the opera-going public enjoy if the Met's four flanking approaches were known as Caruso Street, Nellie Melba Avenue, Antonio Scotti Passage and the Boulevard Schumann-Heink! Would it outrage the residents of Washington Square if the last few blocks of Fifth were rechristened Henry James Avenue? And would it seem inappropriate if the Players Club side of Gramercy Park became Edwin Booth Street with a John Drew and a Booth Tarkington corner? And since the New York Herald has long since lost its identity in the Tribune, wouldn't it be a happy idea to substitute George M. Cohan Square for Herald? Paris has vehicular tributes to her humorists (Courteline, Alphonse Allais, etc.) and to her popular illustrators (Steinlen, Willette, etc.). How it would lift the heart to note that the corner sign near the Algonquin had been changed from 44th to Robert Benchley Street and that a similar transformation had taken place a few yards away where 43rd had happily become Helen Hokinson Street.

The theatre district, of course, could be rife with names as bright as its lights. Where Broadway forms a southeast angle with 40th, the name of Maude Adams on one side and on the other, that of Charles Frohman would remind the public that here for sixty years stood the most elegant theatre of America, while other sections would bear happy witness to the fallacy of Garrick's gloomy contention that "an actor's name is writ in water."

Such speculation might even reach the point of starting a civic movement in favor of such rechristenings.

Not, of course, that it would make the slightest impression on whoever is responsible for the naming of our streets (who, incidentally, is?). Nor, probably, if the impression were to be made and the signs eventually changed, would it affect the majority of the New York public. It has been years since 6th Avenue underwent a change of title and how many of us ever refer to it, or even think about it as the Avenue of the Americas?

"It's Ridiculous"

"It's Ridiculous"

MUCH of the charm of the little Latin Quarter hotel where I stayed last summer was due to the fact that most of the bedroom windows faced onto a quiet old courtyard . . . making for a certain degree of coziness among the clientèle. One could look directly down and ascertain how many *croissants* the old academician consumed with his *petit déjeuner*, or directly across and judge whether the Britishers had been out late the previous night, by the hour they started dressing, or directly up to the roof-slates and follow the progress of the hotel cat's romance with the neighborhood tom. One could also hear much of the conversation that went on at the reception desk . . . especially if it went on between the lady concierge and the sort of American tourist who suffers the interesting delusion that the best way to make himself understood in French is to talk English slowly and at the top of his lungs.

One such linguist I overheard of an afternoon in the throes of despatching an air-mail letter. He was the sort of globe-trotter who regarded any custom not 100% U.S.A. in the light of personal affront and the nation who practices it in a state of primitive barbarism. His particular ire at the moment was aimed at the French postal system. For the concierge to go through the leisurely mechanics of first producing a small scale and weighing his letter with the studiousness of an alchemist, then opening out a sort of scrap book from whose pages she extracted the correct postage in stamps, carefully noting the amount in a two-column ledger before finally sticking them onto the envelope . . . all this seemed to him an elaborate waste of time. But when he caught sight of the box in which his letter was deposited, he let out, in tones which in Indiana would have summoned a hog, "You don't call that thing a *mail*-box? It's ridiculous!" The object of his contempt was a little cast iron affair modestly attached to a side of the desk. It indeed looked more like a Victorian child's bank than a receptacle for post. Its only identification was the word "Dépêches" in quaint letters tastily entwined with vineleaves. In halting but soothing English the lady concierge agreed that yes perhaps the box was small but then, que voulez-vous, the district post office was close at hand and there were eleven pick-ups a day. "Eleven?" continued our bigger and better citizen

"We have four! But you should see our mail-boxes!" and he made the gesture of a fisherman lying about a tarpon. Madame, for whom the sight of a U.S. mailbox was not a major ambition, shrugged politely and explained that ah, but with frequent pick-ups the postman had less of a load, the risk of losing any letter was minimized and mail could be despatched with greater frequency. Having no immediate answer, our compatriot uttered another "It's ridiculous!" in tones of finality and walked off in the righteous manner of someone who has just delivered an Arbor Day address.

The incident was hardly one of international import. Nor was the phrase one of significance like "Remember the Maine" or "Lafayette, we are here," but it started to ring in my head, perhaps because I heard it uttered so frequently by certain of my fellow countrymen. (I stress the word *certain* because, thank our lucky stars and stripes, we don't all appreciate France solely for such amenities as "l'American drug-store," "Le Quick Lunch" and night-spots which advertise "Le Jazz hot"!) The unfortunate thing is that the remark is made in tones loud, clear and unmistakable, those who make it going either on the theory that the French, like wax-works or animals in a zoo, are incapable of understanding human comment, or that if they do understand, it doesn't in the least matter. And this seems strangely inconsistent with our national trait of wanting desperately to be liked. For certainly Mr. Average American sets greater store by demonstrations of affection than any living creature with the possible exception of the cocker spaniel. And yet this staunch spoke of the Rotarian wheel, at home so anxious to win friends and influence people he even establishes institutions to impart the higher technology of jolly-good-fellowship, can become a curious paradox in Europe. All too frequently, he stores his courteous behavior back in the States along with his winter coat and becomes a self-appointed ambassador of ill will. We ourselves are among the founders of the "Let's hate America" club and this is a lamentable misunderstanding on everyone's part, for we are basically a warm and friendly people. And yet to judge by some of us we appear to be in a chronic state of impatience, irascibility and . . . I started to say arrogance, but arrogance implies a certain degree of the grand manner which Mr. Tourist-in-Paris has not as he tramples slap-happily over our already ticklish international relations.

If I speak specifically of our behavior in France, it is because I have a feeling it is worse there than in, say, England or Italy. The warm geniality of the Italians disarms even those of our citizens staunchly determined to regard the citizens of other countries as "foreigners" and therefore suspect. And there is something about the British which, whether we admit it or not, tends to subdue the bad child in all of us. The French, on the other hand, have a quality peculiarly riling to the overly Yankee-doodled, and that is an utter self-sufficiency best summed up in their own term of "Je m'en fiche-ism," or "Don't give a damn-ism." (and if you want to be less refined but more accurate, you change the *fiche* to *foute*, which means inserting a God before the damn). This is the Gallic live-and-let-live as opposed to our live-and-let-live-as-long-as-you-do-it-our-way attitude. And if the way isn't ours, even if it works entirely to the satisfaction of the French, for us it's either as hilarious as a moustache-cup or it's an insult to the superiority of American gadgetry and in either event, "It's ridiculous!"

One hears the querulous phrase reiterated concerning the countless things that are "different." The elaborately artistic money. The unelaborate and anything but artistic plumbing. That interesting morning brew which to the French is coffee and to the American the equivalent of ipecac. The casual system of checking a trunk when, in lieu of a baggage tag, a limp little stamp is slapped somewhere on the top and somehow the trunk turns up at its proper destination. The peculiar appearance of French hand-written numerals which more resemble notes of ancient music than figures (I overheard one disgruntled lady telling a waiter "Votre figure est affreuse," which, meaning "Your face is awful," didn't further international relations either). It's all ridiculous!

One even hears the comment in those small, unpretentious restaurants where, in order to save laundry costs, paper tablecloths are used. The napkins, however, are those magnificent king-size ones of heavy linen, a bit rough, always slightly damp and smelling deliciously of hayfields and sour bread. Here for our practical Yank is yet another ridiculous. If they're economizing with paper mats, why not paper napkins? The why-not is obvious to the native habitué of the small restaurant to whom the refinements of the palate are of greater importance than the refinements of fancy table-manners. With happy *insouciance* he opens out the great square, ties two corners about his neck and spreads the rest, like a barber's cloth, out over paunch and lap . . . the ostensible reason being to protect his clothes from flying culinary items, but the more innate one being the anticipatory effect of the gesture, the feel, the smell which serves as a spiritual *apéritif* to that most essential of Gallic blessings . . . "*bon appétit.*" For a Frenchman to trade his beautiful big linen napkin for a flimsy bit of coffee-shoppe frippery is as unthinkable as that he'd trade his red wine and Chateaubriand steak for a milk shake and tuna-fish salad.

Which alimentary subject brings to mind one of the most constant grounds for American incomprehension . . . the two-hours-for-lunch ritual, even though this pleasurable respite is to the French far more vital than television is to us and, thanks to the leisurely habit, there are hardly any stomach specialists in France and ulcers as rare as bubble-gum. If to us the fact that a French businessman would put off an important deal rather than curtail this two hour interval is absurd, just so, to the French, it seems even more absurd that the U.S. prototype would remain tied to his desk at noon, talk on three telephones and dictate a dozen letters while he downs milk from a wax container, a sandwich from a paper bag and calls it a meal. The protracted luncheon hours, like those other lengthy ones spent at the marble-topped table of a pavement café, serenely observing the world through the mellow glow of a single, long-lasting *vermouth cassis*, seem to the more quick-stepping of us a profligate waste of time, that time we are so obsessed with saving . . . a meaningless economy as we so often end up with merely killing it. And here is again a divergence. The French have no such expression as "killing time." In their more philosophical vocabulary the term is "passing time," which means savoring all moments of it each to his individual enjoyment. While we battle with time, they relax with tempo. It is not without reason that one of their writers said "The pleasures of a people reveal their soul" and that the juke-box has yet to rend the air of the quiet *bistro*.

One sure-fire spark-plug for the "It's ridiculous" explosion is when our American is confronted with unfamiliar rules and regulations. When, for instance, he is venturesome enough to risk the hazardous business of driving a car about the city of Paris. He may perhaps have parked on a street where there is no visible interdiction to do so. On returning to his *voiture* and finding stuck under his windshield wiper a communication beginning with a polite "Monsieur," ending with the distinguished salutations of the police department and informing him he has violated the rules of stationing himself, he becomes righteously indignant. The indignation reaches Olympian heights when, on tracking down the gendarme who made out the ticket and demanding the reason for it, he is told that obviously, as everybody knows, on the odd days of the month, one parks on the odd number side of the street . . . on even days, on the even number ones . . . a regulation which to our hero is so preposterously cockeyed, it robs him of all expletive speech except an apoplectic "It's ridiculous!" This is an ill-advised bit of self-expression for the Paris gendarme is no more appreciative of civilian criticism than is the New York cop. He can, however, become the most lenient of constables when approached with the proper technique, which is to look helpless, speak with meek politeness and admit to being a barbaric foreigner ignorant of local rules.

Such appeal to the Gallic sense of reason usually does the trick and chances are, the toughest officer will dismiss his belligerence with a twirl of his white baton and end up by delivering, instead of a ticket, a discourse on the logical beauties of Parisian traffic laws, explaining that an ordinance such as this one of parking on odd or even sides of the street according to the odd or even days of the month is in the interests of the shop-keepers who thereby take turns sharing the handicap of a line of parked cars blocking their doorways. Of course, if the offending driver is a woman and not bad-looking, she may resort to the more fundamental technique used by a friend who having failed at a rotary crossing to drive to the right of the indicators was hauled up by an outraged gendarme. As he thrust his face in through her window, she smiled with pretty apology and, in a gesture of fluttering femininity, clutched to her cheek a highly perfumed handkerchief, whereat the "flic" melted, sniffed the air with the ecstatic appreciation of Ferdinand the Bull, sighed "Ah Madame, que vous sentez délicieuse!" and gallantly waved her on.

One sometimes wonders how often the French, observing us, say (tactfully out of our earshot of course) "C'est ridicule!" What about the dollar-laden spenders of the Right Bank de luxe caravanseries whose motives in coming to Paris are purely material . . . the material ranging from the satin of a Dior gown to the canvas of a Miro abstract, the sort who when being told a price in francs ask "How much is that in *real* money?" who have given rise to the Left Bank quip that the reason for the scaffolding on the tower of Saint Germain-des-Prés is that a rich American has purchased it and is having it crated for shipping? And speaking of that pastoral saint who keeps what must be an astonished watch over today's student quarter, what about our opposing types on this opposing bank? The sort who swell the ranks of these mid-century "incroyables," the espousers of what the French call the "snobisme de la purée," a snobbism of the slovenly . . . which makes one want to rename the district "Saint Germain Depraved" . . . the free young untidies, slopping about the streets of France's capital strolling through the Louvre or into Notre Dame in clothes they'd never dream of wearing at home outside the workshop of a summer-stock playhouse. What about the genial drunk I saw get up in a cabaret and start coaching the orchestra which wasn't up to his Dixieland standards? Or the less genial lady visiting the flea market whom I overheard (as indeed did everyone within a block) proclaiming to a friend "Of course these Frogs jack up their prices as soon as they see an American because there's something mean and sneaky about every one of them!" And what about one more conjecture? What if the situation were reversed and we in America were in the yearly position of being invaded by French tourists who treated us with similar insensitivity and our native mores with similar contempt? How long before we'd be protesting violently in the press and scrawling on our walls whatever would be our version of the "U.S. GO HOME" signs!

The sagest advice regarding tourist conduct came from a gentleman himself a Frenchman, living in a large mid-Western town where he fulfills consular function for his country and at the same time conducts his own private business whose main offices are in France. Rather than make repeated trips over and back during the year, he arranges for his associates to fly here for their conferences. Realizing that for those of his countrymen who have never before journeyed beyond the borders of La Belle France the transition from the airport at Orly to one in the heart of Ohio may come as a bit of a shock, he meets them on their incoming plane with a warm greeting and words which go something like this: "Listen, mon vieux. You're in the United States of America. You'll find that some things are a lot better here than *chez-nous*, some things a lot worse and some things . . . just different. You'll even find that the food is edible . . . some actually delectable. But it won't be France, and while you're here it won't do any good to complain. Accept the situation and you'll have a good time. If you can't, you can always remember that the trip is temporary and you'll soon be back home." It is my belief that a short transcript of these sentiments should, along with the vaccination certificate, be compulsorily enclosed with every American passport.

Your Very Good Health

Your Very Good Health

O NE of the more inexplicable characteristics of homo not too sapiens is his intolerance of his fellow man's eating preferences. That food has always been, and will continue to be, the basis for one of our greater snobbisms does not explain the fact that the attitude toward the food choice of others is becoming more and more heatedly exclusive until it may well turn into one of those forms of bigotry against which gallant little committees are constantly planning campaigns in the cause of justice and decency. I personally would not be averse to heading an anti-food-defamation league whose slogan would read "Eat and Let Eat," my zeal for such humanitarian endeavor arising from the fact that for a number of years I have been a member of a misunderstood minority and, in the eyes of an unfeeling majority, a gastronomic pariah. My seeming offense against society has been Yogurt. For years I have been eating Yogurt . . . patiently, doggedly, in spite of the contemptuous amazement of epicurean friends and the boorish catcalls and groans of my loved ones. If Yogurt were on the list of a dietary regimen, I might be spared the censure, but the fact that I eat it for the uncomplicated reason that I like it, is conduct neither to be understood nor forgiven . . . especially by my immediate family. They being violently antipathetic toward most dairy produce, regard Yogurt (which, needless to say they have never so much as tasted) with the horror they have for buttermilk and on what few occasions I have had the misguided temerity to ask them just to try a small spoonful, they have reacted as though I had asked them just to try a small spoonful of crankcase oil. My fondness for the stuff, they consider a family shame like ether-sniffing or the secret tippling of elderberry wine. As a persecuted pioneer (I was, I believe, among the first American Yogurt espousers) it is gratifying after all these years to note the ever increasing popularity of this modest comestible and now when even our rural grocer stocks it, I feel the barriers of prejudice are down and one can proclaim oneself a Yogurt fancier without it having the stigma of proclaiming oneself a Mexican dirt-eater.

This brave candor emboldens me into making a further clean breast of things and admitting that I occasionally like the sort of provender which comes under the distressingly therapeutic heading of "Health Food." I stress the word *occasionally*, for a steady diet of the stuff would be unthinkable. But about once or twice a month the craving for carrot juice gets the better of me and I can't pass by a vegetable-bar without stopping, retracing my steps and ducking stealthily inside. There is something a trifle shame-making about walking deliberately into one of these hygeian estaminets . . . like walking deliberately up to a news-stand and purchasing a copy of "Horoscope" magazine. I find myself glancing guiltily up and down the street lest some gastronomic acquaintance catch me. It would be less awkward if the Health Bar had a discreet Family Entrance for timid outsiders like myself, for I never feel quite at home on the premises. These are usually taken up by a throng of steady customers . . . a strange hierarchy of food cranks who come there in a highly unhealthy pursuit of health, whereas I go there for the simple, if brutish, purpose of eating something which appeals to my appetite. Being a celery and raw vegetable fancier to the extent that I wonder if some early Colonial Skinner didn't once marry a rabbit, I revel in their "nature's salad" and wax mellow after a double "fresh garden cocktail." That nut-flavored saw-dust which goes by the bacteriological name of "wheat-germ" I find as tasty as Major Grey found chutney. I even now and then relish (n.b. . . . readers with squeamish stomachs may here skip to the ensuing paragraph) as a *sauce piquante* for that old weakness Yogurt, a delicate dousing of Black Strap molasses.

For me, a further inducement to the patronage of these vim-imparting eateries is their clientèle. The fascinating thing about most health food addicts is the fact that they look so fearfully unhealthy. Some have the pallor of El Greco visionaries; others, the sweetly doomed aspect of Beth in *Little Women*, while a few give the impression of having gone a third of the way through their analysis and were brooding whether or not to keep on with it. These are the zealots whose attitude is that of being dedicated to a Cause which lifts them above the grosser herd. Food for them would seem to come in the line less of enjoyment than of purposeful duty, as, with quiet fortitude, they munch their bran or soya bean, their eyes turned worshipfully to the framed photograph of Gaylord Hauser hanging above the vitamin counter. Beside these pallid regulars, there have always been a sparse scattering of far less interesting steadies. These are the hearties, aggressive with well-being. Most of them are women, ruddy-cheeked, blondish and speaking with North European accents. They stalk in on massive shoes, bringing with them a regular cold front of fresh air and an attitude that they are the exterminators and the rest of us are cockroaches.

Not all the faithful do their eating on the premises. Some prefer the cash and carry system. They come regularly, on the dot of a certain hour and have only to nod to the vegetable-jerker for that employee to enquire "Will it be the usual?" and, not waiting for reply, to start loading the electric dejuicer with the raw ingredients of "the usual" which trickles greenly forth into a waxed container and is subsequently carried off by the customer with the happy expectancy of Paddy toting away his Saturday night growler.

Such, up until a year or so ago, has been the habitual clientèle of these hygeian snackeries. However, ever since the glamorous European diet authority started telling club ladies how to look younger and live longer, the rapidly increasing presence of a lot of fairly normal seeming patrons is destroying the picturesque character of the places. What's more, there are some mighty swank bistros springing up around town. One in particular attracts a luncheon crowd proportionate to the pre-matinée jam at Sardi's. An unpretentious establishment, it looks, on first inspection, like a combination soda-fountain, pharmacopoeia and the grocery section of Hammacher Schlemmer. The eating department occupies half of the store space with small-table or lunchcounter service. The other half is given over to the sale of canned or packaged foodstuffs and a galaxy of bottled vitamins running the gamut of complex from *a* to whatever letter they stop at. The general décor is one of glass, white paint and chromium. The only interruptions to the spotless wall surfaces are two framed works of art. One is a handsome color photograph of a fruit salad, enlarged on a scale as mammothly frightening as those Kodak blow-ups in the Grand Central Station. The other is a bright study of a young lady poised on a bathroom scale, clutching about her nude midriff a turkish towel, one foot delicately extended as if testing the temperature of some unseen water but actually, with one shell-pink toe, pointing to a box of goodies known, I regret to say, as "Slim Tays-Tees." There is, of course, the Hauser votive shrine. Here the likeness of the good green doctor is perched on a shelf given over to special salubrious cosmetics . . . soaps, cold-creams, toilet-waters and lotions made, one assumes, from the purest of herbs, the most beneficial of spices and the tuberculin-tested milk of wild asses.

You may eat at one of the ice-cream parlor tables for four . . . which is awkward as it means sharing the board with three unknowns who are apt to watch your every mouthful. I find it preferable to perch Drama Quartette fashion on a stool before the highly therapeutic counter. Except for the electric dejuicer and the piles of raw vegetables, this looks pretty much like any tidily kept lunch counter. There are the usual napkin holders and the usual containers of drinking-straws. There are also the usual bowls and shakers . . . but don't for a minute be fooled into thinking that what's in these last is in any sense usual. Woe to the guileless neophyte who sprinkles the contents of the shakers over his cottage cheese only to discover that instead of pepper he has doused it with cinnamon sugar, and, in the place of salt, a mineral substitute resembling bacon flavored beach sand. Beware also of dumping into your coffee a spoonful from the sugar bowl. Like as not it will turn out to be wheatgerm. Moreover, if you commit any of these boorish errors, the regulars, who are offensively in the know, will shake their heads with pity while the waitresses will stare incredulously as though you had started in combing your hair with one of the plastic forks.

Further uptown is a smaller, less snooty establishment which I vastly prefer. The proprietor, a cheery soul who is also the meal preparer, waiter and juice-*sommelier*, seems delighted and not a little amazed when a customer walks in. He dishes up the orders with alacrity and presides over each mouthful with friendly interest. His is a personality partly Scout-master, partly non-proselyting missionary. He seems to assume that if one is not already a health-food true believer, one's conversion is imminent. I always have the uneasy feeling that he's going to hand me out a tract along with the check. Fortunately he hasn't so far. There is, however, ostentatiously displayed on the far end of the counter a pile of publications which I hesitate to scrutinize too closely for fear he'll talk me into a subscription. They bear such titles as "Let's Live," "Health in Mind and Body" and one which a faulty eyesight led me to believe was "Superman News" but which a second glance made out to be the latest official chit-chat of the Supermarket. Other reading matter . . . and even more fascinating . . . is to be found on the labels of certain canned stuffs geometrically pyramided back of the counter. Apart from the routine dietary vegetables which have been vitamin-enriched, chopped, strained and generally mal-treated, there are any number of somewhat astonishing substitutes for meat . . . vegetarian versions of Spam. They are touted as being delectable, invigorating and seemingly just the meal ticket for everybody from Olympic champions to convalescents and the late George Bernard Shaw. There is something called Yum . . . which, to judge by the picture on the label, would be an ersatz meat loaf, and there is something called Proast which I suppose with a highly active imagina-tion and the sort of head-cold which anaesthetizes the taste-buds might vaguely resemble hash, and there are some strange things called Choplets which appear to resemble nothing but themselves. There is also a com-modity known, with the archness of "near-beer," as "Not-Meat." Whether there is a big market for these staples among the faithful, I wouldn't know. The geo-metric symmetry of the pyramid seems to remain the same.

Of all the health food emporiums, the early ones were much the most appealing. A block or two from where I live was a modest shrine to Hygeia which for me held infinite charm. A narrow hole in the wall, its eating facilities were limited to a counter just long enough to accommodate four patrons who were care-ful not to stick their elbows out too far. The remainder of space was given over to merchandise shelves sparsely stocked with a few boxes of lime-blossom tea, paper-bound books concerning diabetes, blood-pressure and longevity, and some jars of a special honey, so rarefied, it would seem to have been concocted on Mt. Hymettus by radio-active bees. On the wall were some very handsome hand-painted notices of the *spécialités* of the *maison* reading "Like a Soyabeanburger?" and "Try our Kanana Banana." At the back of the shop, behind a curtain fashioned from a Navajo blanket was a kitchenette of sorts and someone named Viola who concocted the salads and, I suppose the Soyabeanburgers. All one ever saw of Viola was a gaunt portion of arm as, silently, she passed the orders out around the Navajo blanket to the proprietress. This lady looked as though, in running a snack bar . . . even a therapeutic snack bar, she had missed her calling. Clad always in peasant blouse, batik scarves and ropes of amber beads, the fortune teller's globe seemed more up her alley than the electric vegetable mixer . . . albeit she lacked the robustness of the conventional Madame Flora. Wan and frail, she looked as if you could knock her over with a camomile leaf. I'd usually find her sitting back of the counter intent on the perusal of a book whose title I never saw but whose content I felt sure was of an occult nature. Seeing me, she would, with great reluctance, put down the volume, having first inserted an Italian leather bookmark. Then, with a soft sigh, she'd rise and with a vague Lady of Shallot smile would drift in my direction and liltingly enquire, less of me than of some being of the upper air, "May I help you?" My impulse was always to reply "May *I* help *you?*" but instead I'd voice my fancy for a double vegetable juice.

"The special?" she'd sing.

"The special" I'd counterpoint, not having the remotest idea what it meant. With an expression of sweet fortitude, she'd don a pair of rubber gloves many sizes too large for her. Dangling off her bird-like hands, they used to remind me somewhat gruesomely of a clown's false feet. Why she went to such lengths of sanitary precaution, I can't imagine, for she never so much as touched gloved finger to frond of parsley. Taking up a pair of tongs, she would gingerly pick the carrots, spinach *et al* out from a square glass tank originally intended for the care and feeding of tropical fish, and deftly place them in the electric dejuicer. Hers was a brisk little machine which, as it ground out the ingredients, gave forth shrill sounds as if the carrots inside it were perishing in excruciating agony. Once, in a crazy moment of thinking she might be of a literary bent and listening to the screams of the expiring vegetables, I jestingly quoted the lines from the Bard about the "shrieks like mandrakes torn out of the ground that living mortals hearing them run mad." . . . which I admit was pretty affected of me. The lady's blank stare indicated she thought I must have heard plenty of mandrakes. I explained it was from *Romeo and Juliet,* whereat she smiled politely and shook her head in a "no-speak-Shakespeare" manner and continued torturing the garden greens.

As a barkeep she was a fine hand at a nifty "health cocktail" which she would serve in a paper goblet and setting it before me would enquire "Will there be anything else?" in a tone which presupposed that there couldn't *possibly* be. Shyly I'd ask if I might have a salad. "*The* salad?" she'd ask. "*The* salad," I'd echo. It was a sort of rite. (I never felt I was quite ready to try that Kanana Banana.) Sadly she'd float toward the door at the back and trill "One salad, Viola" . . . with accent on the *o*. The only indication that Viola had heard, or that, indeed she existed, was a slight agitation of the Navajo rug. The proprietress would take a patient stand beside the door, in the mystic attitude of a sibyl waiting for a private message from the oracle. Within a remarkably short time, the gaunt forearm of Viola would manifest itself, shoving the salad in her direction and, bearing it like a votive vessel, the proprietress would bring it to the counter, place it before me; then, returning to her chair, she would rearrange the amber beads, pick up her book, and silence would reign . . . that is if I didn't come too abruptly to the end of my beverage, creating one of those startling suction sounds through the straws. In which case I'd say "Pardon *me!*"; the lady would coo indulgently and again silence.

I was usually the only customer. Now and then a strange, colorless person would drift in for an ethereal snack or the purchase of a jar of that rarefied honey. This product brought out a surprising animation in our hostess. She'd suddenly wax enthusiastically vocal explaining to the purchaser (who was usually the same person) how life-giving it was and how particularly splendid were the bees who produced it. I learned in

155

time that she was not always a dreamy counterpart of the Lady of Shallot. She could, on occasion manifest a gallant firmness of character. I am thinking specifically of the time a dame in a mink jacket teetered in on platform shoes, brandishing an onyx cigarette holder and demanded a cream-cheese sandwich, adding that it *must* be on white bread. "Then," replied the priestress of righteous eating "it *must* be in the soda fountain down the block. I have never allowed a crumb of white bread in my establishment," and with proud dignity, she turned her back to the astonished customer and picked up her book . . . I noted she was trembling slightly.

I got out of the habit of frequenting this recherché little spot . . . frequenting is hardly the word and my occasional patronage was hardly a habit. Only the other day, feeling the old longing for a solitary bout of juice-tippling, I walked down to the old haunt. The place was closed. A "store to rent" sign was plastered across the window. I peered regretfully in through the glass door. The counter was gone, along with the Navajo rug. Only the merchandise shelves remained . . . the shelves which once had housed that magic honey. I thought of the frail little proprietress. It made me sad not to catch a glimpse of batik scarf or rope of amber beads. I wondered what had become of her and rather hoped the kindly bees had wafted her away.

My Life as a Sports Widow

My Life as a Sports Widow

FOR twenty-five years I have been married to a sportsman and being in not the remotest way a sportswoman myself, I have many times experienced the curious and deserted sense of being a sports widow. I daresay that my husband would put it that for twenty-five years he has been married to an actress and that much of the time he, in turn, has felt like a theatrical widower. That, however, would be his story and this is mine.

I consider it a point of honor for my side of the family to state at the outset that I come of people who, though not sporting in the modish sense of the term, were, in all other respects, normal and acceptable. I spent my girlhood in the country for the simple reason that my parents both loved it . . . although they never felt that they must complicate their rustic affection by going in for any athletic organization about it. Mother was an avid gardener . . . which, of course, doesn't count. Father was an avid walker and had been known to scale an Alp or two, but apparently mountain climbing doesn't count either in the animal sporting world.

At the time of my marriage, I was under the cheery impression that, as a physical specimen, I was a healthy if not, indeed, rather a splendid one. I could swim, roller-skate, bicycle and play a nice bad game of tennis. I could even ride a horse, provided it was a kindly Western pack-pony and I was within clutching distance of the pommel. But this last, I soon learned, isn't considered riding. In fact it seemed doubtful if the faithful creature that bore me up Sunset Trail could even be considered a horse.

For at the time of our marriage, my husband's sporting interests centered solely and passionately about horses. Riding them (called "hacking"), employing them for the pursuit of hounds who, in turn, were in pursuit of a fox (called "huntin'") . . . or if the hounds were, in lieu of a fox, in full cry after a bag of annis-seed (called "dragging") . . . observing them at race-meets, judging them at horse-shows, even paying formal calls on them in the stalls of their owners. In a desire to prove a perfect helpmate I tried, as a blushing bride, to go in for the fancy. It was my husband who did the blushing . . . and right at the start when I announced that I too could ride. Why I even had a habit I'd bought when I was at Bryn Mawr . . . a lovely little outfit of tweed knickers, sleeveless jacket and stout army puttees.

With admirable control, my husband agreed that indeed the outfit must be just the thing for Colorado, but not exactly right for the New York or Long Island riding set. Furthermore as I'd be riding side-saddle (an announcement which knocked me for a loop) we'd better see about getting some proper equipment. The seeing was effected in London. An Oxford Street tailor, all covered with "By Appointment" insignia, made me a side-saddle habit so extremely heavy, wearing it I could barely move on foot . . . let alone subsequently on the horse. My boots were from Peale . . . beautiful objects worthy a guardsman and with that rich polish which, it was pointed out, "you can fairly see your face in" . . . although what woman wants to see her face in a riding-boot? None other than the historic firm of Lock & Co. made me my bowler hat. They call it, I believe, *building* you a bowler. It would be more accurate to say that they *cook* you one, for, at the fitting, they bring it forth from some hidden hat-bakery, exuding clouds of steam and clamp it on your astonished head . . . a startling experience for anyone unused to trying on hats the temperature of a plum pudding.

The sum total of all this highly authentic and yet more highly expensive equestrian ensemble was most impressive and I vastly admired my appearance in it.

The admiration, however, failed to be shared by any of the horses I encountered. We just somehow didn't speak the same language and of my riding career it is too humiliating to speak other than to state that it was (mercifully for both horse and rider) short-lived. I abandoned for all time the idea of my picture ever appearing in *The Spur*, divorced myself from any active sports participation and resigned myself . . . well, more or less . . . to becoming a sports widow. That is, to following, from a distance of legal separation, the outdoor enthusiasms of my spouse.

My spectator sporting career might be divided into three periods . . . the horse, the duck and the retriever. During the first part of the horse period, my husband's obsessive delight was fox-hunting. My personal opinion of fox-hunting I have usually had the diplomacy to keep to myself. But there can be nothing undiplomatic in quoting another opinion . . . that of Samuel Johnson. Actually the learned doctor was a good horseman and won the approval of a rural squire who heaped upon him true sportsman's praise when he said "Why Johnson rides as well for aught I see as the most illiterate fellow in England." However Johnson himself summed up the pastime with "It is very strange and very melancholy that the paucity of human pleasures should persuade us ever to call hunting one of them." Never having tasted the heady intoxication of being mounted in the field with hounds in full cry, I cannot vouch for the sportsman's reply to this pronouncement. But from this spectator sportswoman's point of view I'd say that the crotchety old sage never spoke words more true.

Having abandoned any hope that his wife might in time be what I believe is called "a fine woman to hounds" (meaning not that she pats the hounds, but that she chases after them on horseback) my husband had, perforce, to accept the paltry solace that at any rate I could go along with him for a few week-ends to upper New York State where there was a hunt of which he was a member and enjoy the privilege of observing the goings-on. These took place in a stretch of hill and valley which I, in my crude verbiage, would have called lovely farming land but which, I was informed, was "good galloping country." And the sight of it causes sportsmen to look virile, dilate their nostrils and start dropping their final *g*'s.

It was during the first stern initiatory week-end that I learned certain hard and fast rules of the world of sports . . . those activities, that is, involving man versus animal or bird. Any and every one of these in order to qualify as first class must involve a certain amount of acute physical discomfort, not the least of which is an excruciatingly early morning arising. All worth-while sporting events must start at break of day . . . which means that all participants must get up and dress a good two hours ahead of the break . . . a period when any vestige of heat in private home, country inn or motel is non-existent. Such purposeful physical exertion has upon your true sportsman (and he's yours, not mine) an exhilarating effect of possessing spectacular courage akin, I sometimes think . . . to the attitude of those exhibitionists who go swimming on New Year's at Atlantic City.

Lacking the proper response to the exhilaration, I found it a matter of acute pain to shiver into my clothes in a dark and glacial room. And subsequently the pain turned to fury when I found out that I might have remained in bed much longer than my husband. For it takes a hunting gentleman a great deal of time to get into the proper attire for a proper member of a proper hunt.

Why people who are about to encounter all manner of clothing hazards from horse sweat to flying mud, not to presuppose the waters of a ditch into whose slimy depth they are not unlikely to be hurled, or even the grimmer possibility of their own life's blood, should dress with the meticulous care of a foreign minister about to attend a court levee, I don't know. But I do grant that there is something of the grand manner about it . . . like the Bourbon aristocrat taking a pinch of snuff while mounting the steps of the guillotine. And I must admit that my husband resplendent in white britches, gleaming boots, impeccable stock and red . . . (I said *pink!*) coat, mustard vest and that squire's version of the crash helmet, a reinforced silk topper, looked as pretty as a British Christmas card. I felt that I really "belonged" . . . if only by proxy, as we drove to where "hounds were meeting." Horses were also meeting and also human beings . . . but they are never mentioned, owing, doubtless, to the natural modesty of the hunter . . . and also that of the horse.

For the non-participant, there are several methods of following a fox-hunt. One may tag along at a distance on a horse. One may dash on foot via frantic short-cuts to various points which it is to be hoped will be viewing ones. Or one may pursue a zig-zag course, equally speculative, through side-roads and lanes in a car. Needless to state which method this one employed. Our car was a convertible and my concession to sport was to keep the top open, even when it was raining.

On arriving at that first meet, it was a relief to discover that I was not the only decadent to follow the hunt from behind a steering wheel, for quite a number of other cars were also there and waiting in line. To be sure, their occupants looked to be elderly folk, or women about to have babies, or hunters and huntresses who only the previous week had smashed a few bones on the field of honor and had now heroically emerged to witness their friends do the same. There is a cheery flow of chumminess between these hunt followers. Although you may never before have met, the moment you take your place in the line-up, everyone nods and waves and laughs . . . over what you don't quite know. The hunt starts and so does the motor line, again amid nods, waves and snatches of laughter and led always by some expert who claims to know for certain which direction the fox will take. You re-assemble for what is called a "check" . . . a sort of time out for

horses, hounds and (or so I always secretly hope) the
fox . . . and again the followers exchange cheery
salutes. You continue to do so passing one another on
the road and if an enthusiast's bumper happens by
accident to bash into your mudguard, the incident is
to be passed off as a mere gesture of camaraderie, like
a hearty pat on the back.

Whoever has witnessed the spectacle of a fine fox-
hunt need not be reminded of its excitement and
beauty. Nor is mine the intention of adding to the
vast amount already written on the subject. However,
lest anyone assume that a non-sportswoman is callously
unfeeling, let me go on record to say that the sudden
weird sound of that melancholy little horn has turned
my hair to electric wires and that the sight of horses
with their bright-coated riders streaking across a slope
or of hounds streaming in a yelping torrent out of an
autumn copse, has caused me to bawl like a baby.

Thrilling as one's first view hallo may be, repetition
of the same performance for hours on end and day
after day can make for satiety and the thrill ceases to
keep pace with either horses or car. I gave myself an
honorable discharge from the mechanized hunt-
followers corps after a certain near-disaster. This occurred one week-end when I had brought my father
along to give him a taste of the bracing life into which
his daughter had wed. With that show-off authority
of someone who with only the vaguest knowledge of
a subject explains its intricacies to someone who knows
absolutely nothing about it, I gave him a running com-

mentary offensively peppered with a few of the highly technical terms I'd only recently picked up . . . how hounds were "giving tongue" or how the fox was about to "break cover" and other colorful John Peel-isms.

I had, meanwhile, swung out of the motor-car line and taken a small side road, my reason being, I said, that I thought the fox would go "down wind." Sheer bravado on my part. I had no more idea of which way the wind was blowing than what down it meant. Father made the politely attentive face that showed he wasn't listening then suddenly went tense and cried "Watch out! You're going to hit a dog!" A lean, furry animal was darting past the front wheels and only a violent jamming on of brakes prevented its death. As it scuttled into an adjacent field my father commented that it was a peculiar looking collie. Then we paused in wild surmise, caught breath and gasped in unison "Good God! It's the fox!" We watched it lope easily away to safety then, both of us being underground members of the Animal Resistance, shook hands and never told a soul. What would have happened had I run over the creature is a supposition too frightful to dwell upon. I should certainly have had to leave the community, if not the state and, in all likelihood, my husband.

And while we're on horses . . . which, thank heaven we are not . . . there are other equine activities which over the years have forced me into the state of sports widowhood. I don't count horse racing which

I happen vastly to enjoy. But I do count horse showing which I happen vastly not to. Needless to argue the pros and cons of this form of public spectacle. Some people hate the opera. Some hate horse shows. The opera hater should not be obliged to sit through an uncut presentation of *Parsifal* and I long ago revolted against sitting through a similarly uncut presentation of horses . . . horses, nothing but horses . . . not even an occasional zebra and observing them as they walk, trot, canter, jump and stand still.

I tried. I really tried. My husband who did a lot of judging in those days suggested that perhaps if I were to go along with him and watch him judge, I'd acquire a taste for the thing . . . like olives. Watching a horse judge at work has somewhat of the static quality of watching a chess champion at play. There are long, long periods when absolutely nothing seems to be happening. The horse show judge stands in the center of the ring . . . most of the time quite motionless. Occasionally he tells someone who tells the riders who in turn tell the horses when to vary their routine. Occasionally he makes mysterious notations on a pad and occasionally he carries on a whispered conversation of a highly secret nature with a co-judge. At last the horses are lined up, their saddles removed and as they stand there in all their nudity, he walks appraisingly around each one, signs something which those who don't win hope is his own death warrant, but which proves to be his final decision, watches the ringmaster attach the ribbons, then he and the co-judge retire for what I enviously presume to be a drink. And there you have the amenities of watching someone officially judge a horse. I made a friendly pact with my husband to the effect that every time he insisted I go with him to a horse-show, I'd insist he go with me to the Museum of Modern Art. It works out very well. I go to Madison Square Garden for the Ice Carnival and his shadow has yet to fall below the Calder mobile.

I daresay that what has chiefly put me off the horse . . . other than the animal itself, is the frightful sense of being amid the alien corn any time I find myself socially amid the horsey set. Especially at one of those swanky rural dinners in a country house where great-grandfather's oil portrait has been replaced by the portrait, also in oils, of the prize-winning stallion, all the flower vases are trophy cups and even the service plates are decorated with views of the Grand National. Not that everyone isn't pleasant in the extreme. They are all of them charming, affable, courteous and often uproariously jolly. It's simply that I don't know how to talk to them. The basis of good conversation, one is taught, is to take a topic and toss to and fro. But I'm damned if you can toss a horse to and fro and the result is that I become mentally paralyzed. In other words, you can lead a horse to Cornelia, but you can't make her think.

I have, however, learned to listen. When my dinner partner traces the ancestry of his special blood-line, I hang on every word as if he were an Egyptologist tracing the line of the Ptolemys. And . . . an even greater social triumph, I can still shriek with mirthful appreciation at every repetition of that joke about the difference between the British and the American hunter and how whereas one calls out "Tally-ho! Gone away!" the other yells "There goes the sonofabitch!"

A coasting accident which resulted in a serious injury ended my husband's riding career, but not my sports widowhood. For after the horse, the wild duck raised its pretty beak.

Again I made a brave attempt to be a helpmate and at the start even went along for one of those "good days of shootin'." And again was brought home to me that basic sportsman's rule of acute discomfort and of early rising in a glacial room. Only duck hunters arise even earlier than fox ones. To such a degree, in fact, it ceases to be even early and becomes simply terribly late the night before. This entails a furtherance of discomfort by having to down, either in your own icy and deserted kitchen or in an over-heated and truck-driver-crowded dog wagon, a nocturnal breakfast which must be traditionally mammoth, despite the fact that only a few hours previously you have eaten a heavy dinner and joined the shooters in toasting the morrow's fun with far more drinks than it could possibly warrant.

On three or possibly four occasions I tasted the primitive joys of deep-freezing from dawn to dusk in a duck blind and never seeing a bird, for not being a "gun" I was always told to get down out of sight and cower in crouching stillness (fingers well stuffed into ears) while the marksmen let fly their volleys and, sometimes, felled their prey. Then again I abandoned any ideas of being an interested spectator sportswoman or even, in this instance, an apathetic decoy. Now when my marital Nimrod and our mallard-minded house guests arise at 3 A. M., I lie in bed. But don't for a minute imagine I'm sleeping. As soon as duck enthusiasts put on their shooting togs, they go into their own special ham act of fearful virility. Their voices even when supposedly subdued become heartily amplified. Moreover they cease to walk and instead they stamp. And as their attire makes them weigh a very great deal, the effect when heard through a closed door is that of a number of young dinosaurs romping about the house.

And speaking of that attire, until I found out that other duck fanciers were the same way about their shooting clothes, I kept secret the horrendous state of those of my husband, as they might have been the family's skeleton in the closet. As a matter of fact, they do have their own closet and as far as the skeleton is concerned, one wonders, upon opening the door, if it isn't that of some long forgotten duck lurking in a distant pocket. My husband is a gentleman of meticulous cleanliness, and so, as far as I can in all propriety make out, are his duck-shooting companions, but it is to me quite incomprehensible why a duck-shooter's garments must acquire the venerable dignity of years and remain undesecrated by dry-cleaning as though they were price-

less fragments of Coptic textiles. Well-seasoned shooting clothes are doubtless delicious to the dog in the
duck blind, but in the evening when the hunter home
from the hill starts warming up over a fire and a few
stiff drinks . . . Oh well, let's leave him by the fire
and go on to the ducks themselves.

During the season, my husband goes out about three
days a week and, being a good shot, always gets his
limit. Personally I for one am all for amending the
game laws and limiting the limit. For although he man-
ages to distribute a fair amount of the trophies among
his duck-eating acquaintances, the overflow remains
with us and our ice-boxes take on the appearance of
storage shelves in a wholesale feather concern. Only
essential staples are allotted a meagre section and all
superfluous delicacies are removed to make way for
the spoils of the chase . . . and sometimes the word
spoils becomes uncomfortably apt. If the weather is
right (meaning I wouldn't quite know what) a few
"brace may be put out to hang." In everyday parlance,
a few pairs dangle like the accessories of a scarecrow
outside the back door until they are "properly hung,"
which is just a day or so before the buzzards start coming up from Southern New Jersey. For a duck should
be approaching a state of fine Stilton in order to suit
the sportsman's palate. And as everyone knows, the
correct way to cook it comprises very little more than
showing it to the oven.

At this point, to my sports widowhood is added the
further austerity of strict diet for, shocking as it may

be to admit, I don't really care for wild duck even if it has remained for some time *in* the oven. I don't care for the vague flavor of fish of which all sportsmen insist it doesn't taste and of which I don't even insist because it just plain does. I don't care for the surgical operation involved in carving it and I don't think that biting into shot is an adventure in good eating. I'm quite sure that it is a hunter's pride which for him adds an Escoffier zest to the meal. I admit that it would for me. If I were able to shoot even an ostrich, I'd eat it and fool myself into thinking it delicious.

Thank God for the game laws which confine this season to three scant months. But there are other months and other games and the latest aspect of my sports widowhood is the retriever trial. We live on Long Island and the retriever trial has taken over Long Island like the tent caterpillar.

Lest there be any extant half-wit such as myself who until recently never knew what a retriever trial was, let me briefly explain that it is an all-day and several days performance at which retriever fanciers gather together with their highly trained animals and put them one by one through a series of tests which involve intelligence, obedience, perception, physical prowess and every virtuosity short of the ability to read Homer in the original. The day is divided into various series, some taking place on land, others on (and in) water . . . events during which birds are either shot in flight, or their extinct bodies are concealed in grass or shore edge and the retrievers one by one at specified signals go forth and with speed and agility retrieve the creatures bringing them back in tail-waving triumph to owner or handler. Sometimes the dog is allowed to watch which way the bird falls. In the case of the concealed one, he must ferret out in a sort of canine treasure-hunt, being directed in this by the handler who from afar blows piercing blasts on a shrill little whistle and goes through an arm waving set of semaphore signals which are retriever code for orders like "Turn right!" "Get back!" "Come forward!" and "Drop dead, you dope!"

Here, I was assured, was one sport I could follow with zest for everyone loves a field trial. The people love it, the dogs love it, even, it would seem, the birds love it . . . although they haven't much time in which to capture the spirit of things.

I tried once or twice to capture it. Here again is one of those long-drawn-out sporting occasions involving an awful lot of waiting about. And you never know what sort of weather you'll be waiting about *in*. For nothing daunts the field trial enthusiast. If it's a question of rain or hail, or heat or snow, or heat or dark of night, he's a rival for any courier on the Post Office building.

There's no denying that the dogs are lovely to watch for a time. But the time can start seeming interminable, and the waits between each of their acts are more drawn out than intermissions at the ballet. Moreover admirable as the animals are, going through their paces, repetition makes for tedium. At first I made shy little attempts to relieve the monotony by wandering in a friendly fashion among the other spectators. But as they are always intent upon the dogs, conversation is out and while a retriever is working out a problem, chit-chat among the humans is bad form. I once made the mistake of going over and scraping acquaintance with certain of the dogs lined up for the next series . . . a gross breach of behavior for which I was severely reprimanded. A retriever about to go on line is like a tenor about to go onto the stage of the Met. You mustn't pat or distract him. You mustn't even pause to say "Hello" or "How's your paw?"

Once again I granted myself a sports divorce . . . this time on the grounds of field trials. Even when some of them are held on our place. These trials are not the big important events, but lesser occasions known as *sanction trials* meaning that when a dog wins, the owner gets congratulations instead of a silver ash-tray while the dog receives an encouraging pat instead of a Ph.D. Our place, it seems, is just right for a sanction trial because, as I was told by one of the judges with kindly approval, "the land is so nice and uncared for."

The opening series starts in a field directly in front of our house. Cars and dog-laden station wagons assemble on a rise a bare sixty yards beyond my bedroom windows. Need I remark that the field trial, like all clean, God-fearing sports, starts at break of day? And a number of the more eager cars start assembling even before the break.

As lady of the land, I thought at first that it behove

me to get up and out and greet the arrivals as they came, but found, to my intense relief that it was not required of me. People intent upon the handling of their dogs don't want to be bothered by any well-meaning but misguided hostess hospitably burbling "Do step into our poison-ivy!" Then, I conceived the idea of having coffee on hand in the kitchen . . . but again the fanciers can't be bothered. As one lady enthusiast explained, she just didn't dare pause because she was "running in the open."

So I, not unwillingly, remain indoors. Someone has to stay there anyway to comfort our house dogs, two Norwich terriers and a small mutt, all of whom start quaking at the first crack of a shot gun and continue in an all-day state of terror. The mutt keeps jumping up into my lap for sanctuary while the elder and supposedly more intrepid terrier hides cowering behind the water-closet. They all three periodically throw up.

The solution, I find, is to betake myself and house dogs off to a cabin we have a few miles away overlooking the Sound and spend a serene or non-gunshattered day. For me there are books to browse through and never quite read, for the dogs there are rabbits to chase after and never quite catch and for us all there is the delight of picnic lunch followed by swinish sleep. In the late afternoon, we return home to find the field trial over and the house crowded with happy sportsmen, shedding wet clothes, getting into dry ones, trying to locate lost car keys, phoning to tell children Mummy and Daddy may be a little late and to go on with dinner . . . everyone drinking and talking at once and nobody listening to a word anyone else is saying. I grab a glass and join in the hearty fun. No one has even noticed my previous absence and everything works out as merry as a marriage bell.

There are worse states than that of sports widowhood. As a matter of truth, I frequently find it to be rather a blessed one.

Hearing Voices

Hearing Voices

LT COMES as an interesting shock suddenly to discover in oneself some eccentricity of behavior which one may have had for years without ever before being aware of it. Take voices, for instance. I find, to my fascination, that many persons, myself in particular, have a curious collection of varying voices, and with the rapt intentness of a Joan of Arc listening to her heavenly sounds, I've been tuning in on my own and other people's earthly ones.

By varying voices, I don't mean accents in their infinite variety, for certainly the contagion of regional pronunciation is too prevalent to be at all a phenomenon . . . especially for those of us who are over-equipped with parrot hearing. I myself return from a trip through the South with an accent of Georgia peach-fuzz, a week in the Middle West and "r's" start rolling their own, while twenty-four hours in London finds me as British as a Trafalgar lion given the power of speech.

I refer, rather, to the tone and manner of delivery we use on specific occasions. There is the way . . . or rather, there are the ways in which people address the elderly on meeting them for the first time. It seems to be a universally foregone conclusion that to be advanced in years means *ipso facto* to be advanced in deafness and whoever is presented to, say, a venerable old gentleman goes on the theory that the poor soul is a living replica of Dickens' adder-eared "A.P." the Aged Parent of *Great Expectations* and starts conversing with the poor dear in a deferential bellow. This is an odd assumption for in these days when the modern hearing-aid has become as chic a device as harlequin bi-focals, it should be easy to gather that whoever is not thus fashionably wired for sound can hear perfectly well and in the case of whoever is so equipped, there is no need for yelling into the contraption and adding to the infirmity the injury of a shattered ear-drum.

The other approach to the elderly is the hospital voice of muted concern, the tiptoe murmur used when visiting a friend who has just had a major operation. This is coupled with a note of awe indicating the supposition that to grow old automatically means to grow holy. I have a woman cousin who is a chipper eighty-nine and when I've introduced people to her, I have watched them shake her hand as it might be a fragile bluebell and when they speak, it is with the solemn reverence of addressing a saint not long for this world. Actually the old girl, who is anything but a saint, is about as fragile as a sturdy oak, and when it comes to this world, she's all for it, has probably just downed a double whisky sour and is rarin' to get to the Canasta table.

The same two vocal reactions manifest themselves when certain persons for the first time discover that the individual to whom they are talking is the victim of a physical handicap . . . even if the handicap is one to which the victim is completely adjusted. My husband twelve years ago lost a leg in a coasting accident . . . a misfortune which he regards less as a tragedy then a damned inconvenience. Some people, on learning that his left leg is constructed of wood, will be shocked into going loud-speaker as though the disability had affected his hearing—while others will lower their tone to one of almost inaudible compassion and continue with gentle sorrow in the manner of bidding farewell to Tiny Tim.

Certain variations in voices seem to be peculiar to male behavior. There is, for instance, the tone men use when conversing with captains of ocean liners. Not that one has occasion for observing the behavior of men conversing with captains of ocean liners frequently enough to warrant this being a blanket observation. I just happen to have noticed it on one or two crossings during those distinguished little gatherings when the captain feels obliged to receive a small group of passengers for cocktails in his quarters. The group has been hand-picked by the purser with advices from the main office and the affair is apt to start off on the stilted side. Conversation will usually begin with polite generalities, then gradually the men of the party . . . not the captain himself, but his gentlemen guests, will bring it around to their own personal seafaring experiences, all of a highly colorful nature and as they do their voices will rise to the tone of someone calling out from the crow's nest while rounding Cape Horn in the teeth of a full gale. The weather may be that of Ancient Mariner calm and the setting one of quiet modern luxury, the captain a gentleman of breeding and culture, and yet he is addressed as though he were the skipper of the *Hesperus* about to lash his daughter to the mast. This may arise from a compulsion to put on a show of manliness before someone of such superior maritime experience. Whatever the cause, the slick businessman from Detroit will go bluff and tell, at the top of his lungs, about that time on Lake Michigan when he darn near capsized, the world-traveled publisher will recall a typhoon in the China Sea as if it were at that instant raging outside and even the distinguished Oxford Don will emit the laconic sounds which with him pass as conversation, in the bark of an Elizabethan sea-dog. Pity the trans-Atlantic captain! How he must long for the company of soft-spoken folk who will discuss the latest Alec Guinness film and the best way of forcing crocuses indoors.

Another oral idiosyncrasy peculiar to the male is the looking-forward-to breakfast halloo. Men, for some disturbing reason or other, seem to act ecstatically worked up over the prospect of breakfast. This is particularly true of those bright business boys on Pullman trains at an early hour of a morning when you're in desperate need of sleep. As they march in Indian file through your car, the leader of the vanguard chooses the moment in which he is passing your roomette to call out to the last member of the rearguard in the cry of a lumberjack logging in turbulent rapids "Oh boy! Am I looking forward to that cup of coffee!" a call to the colors which is echoed, or rather amplified, by each member of the doughty crew as one clarions a yes siree what isn't he going to do to those ham 'n eggs, and another wants jubilantly to know what the betting is on old W. G. here having himself a great big stack of pancakes.

Women, I must admit, are not without their own peculiar noises of enthusiasm. Take, for example, the situation of former school or college mates meeting inadvertently after the hiatus of years. . . . That is, if you are able to take it, for when two women of middle years are thrown together and all of a sudden the staggering fact dawns upon them that the one is . . . not surely Mary Smith!!! and the other . . . it isn't possible, Sally Jones!!! the emotion of recognition is expressed in the mounting melodics of gleeful and slightly hysterical sirens . . . and I don't refer to the sort who sat on rocks and lured mariners with dulcet sounds.

Of further vocal eccentricities of the American female, there is the delivery she uses when talking to her own child in the presence of company. If the child is small and the company someone she doesn't know very well, she is all too prone to plunge headlong into a dewy-eyed motherhood act. Employing that maternal jargon rife with the first person plural, she lilts out gently sweet suggestions such as "Isn't it time we went to beddy-bye" while what she'd like to say, and what the child expects her to shrill out, is "You little pain-in-the-neck, get the hell upstairs!" Even when the child grows older her parlance in its presence before a casual acquaintance is still suggestive of a Victorian elocution mistress giving the proper reading of "Birds in their little nests agree." As my own son once rudely summed it up after a brief encounter with some out-of-town friends "For Pete's sake, old girl, when you're talking about me do you have to sing?"

There are a woman's two beauty-parlor modes of speech. The first is that subdued and highly confidential murmur when, while seated at the manicure table in the more public part of the establishment she and the operator in the manner of international spies, their foreheads all but touching, with furtive glances to make sure nobody is eavesdropping, discuss the condition of her nails. The second is the vociferous blare which, the moment she is placed under the dryer brays out with such interesting items as "And what did he do when he found her in bed with the chauffeur?"

The conspiratorial voice is particularly astonishing in that it is used so often on occasions when there is no need for secrecy . . . as in the case of that husband and wife counterpoint duet toward the end of a social gathering . . . the code exchange when the husband rises and in the manner of a second-story man passing the signal to his partner mutters in the direction of his wife "I think we'd better be . . ." and she, cautiously rising, echoes the sinister password "Yes, we'd better be . . ." What should perforce be so hush-hush about making the simple announcement that it's late and they ought to go home, is a point of etiquette which it is doubtful if even Emily Post could explain.

Of the barnyard imitations and birdcalls women employ when addressing household pets, it is almost too embarrassing to speak. My own domestic animal voice is a source of considerable distress to whoever is unfortunate enough to overhear it. A shameless weakness in regard to dogs releases from me a flow of baby talk and babbling assininities and to state in writing the names and endearments I gurgle at my own dogs would be the equivalent of committing myself to a mental institution. The dogs, who are not overly sensitive about such matters, don't seem to mind. But my family, who is, minds very much indeed and I sometimes mind myself, for when talking with man's best friends I am apt to clench my teeth in a primitive demonstration of affection which has twice resulted in grinding the edge off a jacketed tooth. My parakeet voice is also pretty dreadful, being a stream of falsetto soprano, almost as high as the notes of Yma Sumac but somehow giving more the effect of a leaking steam valve or perhaps a fatuous mosquito. This too is in baby jargon. In fact, all domestic animals appear to reduce me to a state of infantilism and I have even heard myself addressing a police horse as though it were swaddled in diapers and cooing in a bassinette.

Other items in my personal collection of voices, however, I find more interesting. There is, for example, my taxi-driver voice. Either it is my lot always to ride in a taxi whose driver is the loquacious type, or I in turn am the type to whom all taxi drivers talk. And I wish they wouldn't. Not that I harbor any prejudice . . . why some of my best friends are taxi-drivers! . . . it's just that I like to make use of the time in transit to catch up on my all too limited magazine reading. It is exasperating in the middle of a New Yorker article to be rudely interrupted with a "How the Dodgers gonna do today?" and to know that the remainder of the trip will be devoted to an exchange of observations regarding baseball, the weather and the Manhattan traffic situation, shouted between front and back seat. Perhaps it's a sense of guilt over my feelings of exasperation as well as an effort to express for my fellow man a friendliness which at the moment I don't in the least entertain, that compels me to conduct my end of the causerie in tones of bright cheer. Or maybe it's a desire to show this honest laboring man what a democratic soul I am to be sure and that come the revolution, he'll find me on the side of the people (that's a joke, Mr. Senator!). Whatever the subconscious motivation, my taxi-driver voice sounds to me horribly like that of a hockey instructress at a Campfire Girls' barbecue.

I am aware that I have other voices of cheer. One full of ersatz sunshine makes its nauseating appearance when I am all of a sudden confronted by the children of my friends . . . young creatures on whom I've not set eyes for years and who, in the interim, have had the lack of tact to grow up. It may be an unwillingness to accept the brow-furrowing fact that they *have* grown up which still obliges me to address them in the goody-goody manner I used when explaining the rules of the treasure hunt in which they participated at my son's thirteenth birthday party. This is the cheerio note you force out when you learn, not without alarm, that your friend's child has been instructed to call you "Cousin" or, even more horrifying "Auntie" . . . the voice which with hypocritical eagerness utters banalities like "How's the new math teacher?" or "Your dad says you're coming along just fine with your surfboard" as though you even listened to the replies. Only a week ago I shared a train seat with an attractive young woman who turned out to be the daughter of former neighbors who had moved from our community some years ago. I didn't recognize her until she introduced herself saying that she was Penelope E. . . . I squirm to recall that I immediately came out with a loudly blithesome "Why Penny *Pen!*" and pumping her hand with splendid vigor exclaimed "Last time I saw you, you were all covered with poison ivy!" What she was all covered with then was discomfort. Obviously she hadn't been called by the distressing nickname in years. However she smiled indulgently and replied politely to my elephantine inquiries as to how was the family and did she enjoy school and mercy it wasn't possible that she had graduated from *college!* She had, and I noted that the book she was reading was an obscure work of Alfred North Whitehead. But from my tone of cozy indulgence it might have been "Five Little Peppers and How They Grew." Shortly Penny-Pen, under pretext of smoking a cigarette, sought refuge in another car.

Another of my voices which falls somewhat into this "splendid" category is the one permeated with forced camaraderie with which I respond to the person who on meeting me instantly starts calling me by my first name. Set me down as a fuddy-dud, but I for one consider this great American habit of calling everyone Tom, Dick and Harriet on initial introduction very much too bad . . . chiefly because it obviates the pleasurable moment which is one of the amenities of ripening acquaintance when it is mutually agreed to go beyond the formal confines of Mr. or Mrs. It would seem, however, that the "call me Al" form of salutation is here to stay . . . especially in the world of radio and television. So when in some broadcasting studio, a complete stranger comes up to me and says "This is your cue, Cornelia" (or Corny, which is fighting language) I try to go palsy-walsy, an act as unconvincing as the average Britisher's imitation of the average American, and answer "O.K., Toots" . . . the

Toots being less to prove myself a buddy than because I don't know his name.

In contrast to this "good egg" utterance is the one of frightful cultivation. This makes its elegant emergence on those rare and impressive occasions of meeting up with extreme blue blood or great erudition, as when in Boston I have sipped tea with a Back Bay dowager who owned a lock of George Washington's hair and knew all about sea-shells, or when in England I twice held converse with the sort of royalty one addresses as "Ma'am," or when once I sat at luncheon next to Professor Toynbee. At such awesome moments mine becomes the voice of refinement carried to the point of refeenment. It is the vocal crooking of the little finger, the adult version of the small girl's pastime of "playing lady." I hear myself coming out with careful niceties of expression, saying "I daresay" for "I betcha" and "Right you are" for "You're darned tootin' " and using the broad *a* on words like "hand."

A similar voice of elegant propriety is my talking-to-other-people's-servants parlance. Servants have always subdued me to the point of meekness and the hired help of others, especially those of the rich and opulent, scare the daylights out of me. This is particularly true when one arrives for a weekend and is met by a specimen of that *rara avis* which, perhaps for the better, is rapidly becoming extinct, the butler, who with ill-concealed distaste picks up one's suitcase out of which is fluttering the torn shoulder strap of an ancient bra; and when the same suitcase is subsequently unpacked

by another specimen also vanishing and equally frightening, the lady's maid, who betrays by a mere flicker
of the lifted eyebrow that she notes the rumpled condition of one's garments, the fact that one's toilet bottles
are leaking and that a box of face powder has burst
open into a pair of suede shoes. At such times the voice
of refeenment comes in handy if only in an effort to
show that beneath these tawdry tatters there beats the
heart of an aristocrat . . . an act of bravura by which,
of course, neither butler nor maid is at all taken in.

A combination of the voice of refinement and the
jolly-good-egg variety comes forth when I find myself
talking with employees . . . that vague miscellany
comprised of doormen, elevator operators, handymen
and the like, with whom one is on a basis of frequent
encounter but negligible familiarity. This variant is
apt to be terribly well-bred and at the same time archly
good-natured. It is also, I fear, interspersed with little
snatches of polite laughter over things that aren't funny
at all. With a merry toss of the head I'll hear myself
emitting gems of gaiety like "Looks as if we may be
getting a little rain . . . ha-ha!" or "Mercy me! Ha! I
can't find my silly old door-key! Ha-Ha!" This is the
audible incarnation of the Helen Hokinson club woman
without the punch line and it's quite unfortunate.

Another locution I have recently discovered is my
doctor voice. Not the confiding mutter used in situations of illness or consultation, but the one I catch
myself using when I meet some of them socially. Due
possibly to a desire to give the impression that I have

no need for his professional services, coupled with an apprehension that if I show any signs of debility he may ask me to stick out my tongue, I talk with great animation in tones vibrant with radiant health, like someone interpreting the role of Hygeia in a physical culture pageant. It's even worse if the doctor happens to be a psychiatrist. I seldom meet psychiatrists and when I do I have the disquieting feeling that the chair I am sitting on is about to let down into a couch and that my every gesture is indicative of deep-rooted neuroses. The result is again that animated delivery of radiant health plus a careful enunciation to show how frightfully normal I am.

However, when it comes to careful enunciation, there is nothing to equal my talking-with-a-foreigner delivery. And I do not refer to someone who speaks only a foreign tongue, with whom one decides the only means of communication is through a bellow of English. I mean the cultured linguist who speaks my language with far greater elegance than I. If through the perfection of his Oxford verbiage, there comes the slightest hint of foreign accent, I slow down into LP speed, mouthing each syllable with meticulous deliberation and using the basic words of a First Primer. It is the form of painstaking peroration William Penn must have used when explaining his treaty to the Indians.

Of my further vocal idiosyncrasies, there is my chatting-with-clergymen parlance. Be it to my chagrin that the opportunity for chatting with clergymen seldom arises in my secular life, and when it does, I find the situation rather awkward. The sudden sight of a clerical collar at, say, a cocktail party (a sight as rare, I admit, as that of a ruffed grouse) stops me dead in my frivolous tracks. I have the uneasy feeling that at any moment its wearer may call for silence and ask a blessing on the canapés, and if I am introduced to the good man, that, sensing the debased life I lead, he may short wave on high to have me struck down by a thunderbolt. All of which makes me go right into my voice of piety. This is a combination of the hostess of a Cape Cod tea shoppe and Beth in "Little Women," uttered in tones of dignified condolence, hushed and not a little hallowed, as though we were about to step into the next room and view the remains. It is somewhat reassuring to note that other people carry on conversations with parsons in the same funereal manner. It must be one of the more doleful exactions of the dedicated life.

Finally, there is my losing-interest voice, which is less a voice than a fadeout. This creeps slowly upon me during some interminable tête-à-tête with possibly a golf enthusiast or someone just back from Europe and determined to present an unillustrated travelogue, or any other variety of bore. And what issues from my mouth is equally boring because it is quite mechanical. In fact, I have usually no idea what it is saying . . . whether it be lucid talk or variations on eeny-meeny-miney-mo. This is a disturbing thing, for it creates that eerie sensation of standing outside yourself and listening to someone who isn't you at all, but a complete stranger. Yours becomes the detached manner of the ventriloquist listening to his puppet, only the ventriloquist knows what the puppet is saying, while you become more and more surprised over what comes forth from this Doppelgänger of yourself. It's a risky business, this listening to yourself, and one which is making me uncomfortably self-conscious. Perhaps I had better stop enumerating my varying forms of speech. Perhaps, as a matter of fact, in certain situations it might be best for me to stop speaking altogether.

Address to the
American
Gynecological Society

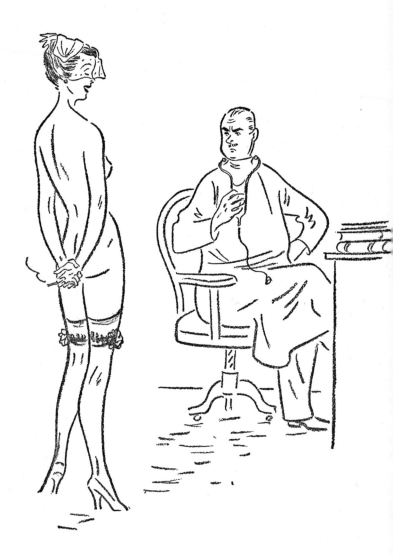

Address to the American Gynecological Society

EDITOR'S NOTE: Miss Skinner has made many speeches at many banquets for all sorts of occasions but she could hardly believe it when she received an invitation to address the annual Convention of the American Gynecological Society at Lake Placid in June 1953. This is a very select group of the country's leading obstetricians and on previous occasions the principal speaker had usually been a distinguished medico who solemnly developed, for the good doctors and their wives on this gala occasion, new horizons in their specialty.

LADIES and gentlemen of the profession . . . if not the oldest in the world, at least one of the most time-honored. You find me in a more awkward position than any in which I have ever been placed by certain of your distinguished members. I am as bewildered by my presence here as you must be. In fact I feel as uncertain of the issue as I did on an occasion when, giving a monologue performance a number of years ago in a New England town, I started off under the handicap of a far from encouraging introduction. (I rather liked this introduction because it is such a fine example of New England's traditional thrift.) The lady of the organization which was . . . having me . . . (that highly obstetrical expression!) rose and with fluttering apology said "Ladies and gentlemen, owing to the high price of Rear Admiral Byrd, we have Miss Skinner with us this evening." Well, let's face it . . . you have Miss Skinner with you this evening and it's not owing to the high price of any of the fees you have charged me over the years.

As I understand it, the yearly address to this learned gathering should be of an instructive or enlightening nature. It is an odd and I must admit a somewhat pleasurable sensation to be in the position of offering advice to the physician.

Well, whether or not you'll take mine, I think this is a golden opportunity for giving the medical profession a bit of the patient's point of view. In other words to hear from the person at the other end of the stethoscope or, in this case, the other end of the . . . shall we say the stereopticon? As the humble presenter of this angle . . . this seldom heard from point of view (I am referring to opinion, not position) I really feel, without undue modesty, that I am a good choice. Over the years I have had the privilege . . . or shall we call it the dubious pleasure . . . of considerable contact with your branch of the profession, due to the fact that *my* profession has obliged me to travel extensively throughout the length and breadth of the United States, and that the birth of a son, plus certain defects of my anatomy, have required frequent consultations, inspections and repairs to the extent that, in the words of Somerset Maugham, you have left me only the bare necessities of life. I have perhaps had more experience than most patients . . . (I'd rather say "clients" . . . the word "patient" immediately reduces me to a state of apprehension and general debility) . . . I have had more opportunities to see you at work . . . if see is what I mean . . . to compare your methods, your relationships with your clients . . . your manners . . . your bedside ones, your desk-side ones and your table-side ones. And I have also had occasion to speculate as to how much you know . . . not of your science . . . but of the point of view of your clientele.

Of course, during your first years of internship you must all have grown callous to the shocks of your profession, but I must tell you (and I am hereby appointing myself spokesman for us beneficiaries of that profession) that we don't easily grow accustomed to such shocks. For the nicely brought-up girl, there is something that is hard to reconcile with her genteel sensibilities about walking into the inner sanctum of a complete stranger, solemnly describing her symptoms and at the end of the recital hearing the stranger say "Will you please go into the next room and take off everything except your shoes and stockings?" It wouldn't seem so bad if it weren't for that shoes and stockings clause! To my impressionable mind it has always smacked of the more erotic refinements of Berlin during its decadence. Be it to the honor of my upbringing, I have always kept on not only my shoes and stockings, but also my hat! If a costume made up of a sheet and a John Fredericks model is not the smartest of attire, God knows it's the most respectable. Even after the sheet has been put to the same sort of use as the old-fashioned photographer's black cloth, the hat remains as the badge of womanly modesty, triumphant over the most distressing of positions.

You know, I married a sportsman. During the first years of married life, I tried valiantly to become a horsewoman . . . a terrifying period which drove me in desperation into becoming a mother. In other words, having learned to put my feet forward into the stirrups, I soon learned the reverse. And from that vantage point . . . those vantage points . . . I had widespread opportunity to observe and compare your varying techniques. I speak, of course, less of medical or surgical techniques than social. It takes all sorts of people to make a world and it takes all sorts of doctors to make a profession . . . (I almost said . . . a patient). There is the frighteningly eminent doctor . . . the sort who is to medicine what Darryl Zanuck is to motion pictures. In other words who is so famous he never appears on the set until everything is made ready for his entrance . . . which is often impressively delayed until the actors begin to wonder if he ever will. And just as you're about to become righteously indignant, he appears, by which time you're in a position in which you can't resist. This sort of doctor is apt to be also the monosyllabic type . . . or even the silent type doctor. During his period of exploration, he never makes a single comment, never utters a word, never smiles, never even goes tchk-tchk-tchk! After the examination he rises abruptly and with noncommittal solemnity, stalks out of the room leaving you with the nurse who tells you that as soon as you've dressed, Dr. Famous will see you in his private office. Of course, you immediately think that what he's found out is so appalling, it defies even the discoveries of Wassermann . . . it's something too awful for even the nurse to hear.

I knew one woman who was finally able to thaw down the cold front of this particularly uncommunicative type. It was around Christmas time, she was very great with child and she was determined to get some sort of response from her dead-pan medico whom we might as well call Dr. Smith. So, with cunning ingenuity she wrote in lipstick across her teemingly fruitful tummy "Merry Xmas, Dr. Smith." Be it to the face-saving credit of the profession that Dr. Smith did laugh.

Then there is the opposite type. The chatty phy-

sician. The sort who asks if you've read any good books
lately or when did you last see the Joneses . . . all of
which would be extremely pleasant if he didn't carry
on such animated chit-chat all the time he's going with
gun and camera into the Heart of Darkness. There's
another fascinating thing about the chatty type. Quite
often it happens that if you run across them socially at
some cocktail party or what have you, they don't recognize you. It comes as quite a shock to discover the
flaw in these genial gentlemen. Maybe theirs is a case of
"I never remember a name, but . . ."

Then there is the singing or crooner type doctor
. . . the sort who in the spirit of Disney's Snow White
whistles while he works. This, I may say, is my favorite type. He shall be nameless but easily recognized
and he's sitting right here in this room. He has a way
of singing while he works . . . which, while most endearing to his clientele who knows and therefore loves
him well, is apt to be a bit confusing to the uninitiated.
My secretary, a wonderful Irish gal, had occasion to
consult him about some one of those minor ills which
a Victorian heritage still obliges us to refer to with
lowered eyes as "a woman's trouble." She listened for
a time to the doctor's cheery vocalizing then looked
. . . down . . . happily at him and said "Glory be
to God, Doctor, you sure love your work." Another uninitiate was the wife of the fine Negro band
leader Count Basie. Mrs. Basie . . . (or should one
say the Countess Basie?) hearing our charming Bing
Crosby of the forceps doin' his stuff, suddenly inter-

rupted him in the midst of his researches to enquire politely "Doctor, just give me that down-beat again."

Now, Gentlemen (I say gentlemen because while I am well aware of the number of feminine members of the brotherhood-sisterhood there are, the harvest of my experience has been gleaned chiefly from the brothers), there is one aspect of your business of which you know nothing whatsoever and regarding which I believe it's high time you were made aware . . . of. And that is what goes on in your waiting-rooms . . . particularly when they are replete with women who in turn, are replete with child. Of course none of you ever pause to see . . . when occasionally you make an impressive dash from your outer door to your inner office—because you're late or because you couldn't face the prospect of looking at us all, or because you've an emergency phone-call, or because you're just plain late. Women in the office of an obstetrician have a behavior all their own. It's a continuous scene of mutual inspection and speculation. One eventually gets accustomed every two weeks or so to seeing the same old familiar faces . . . but the old familiar contours are a constant source of interest far more fascinating than those old copies of Life, Time and the New Yorker which must have been read by all the members of a doctor's family, thumbed up, torn and jumped upon and eventually placed on the table of his waiting-rooms. The obstetrician's waiting-room is the one place of gathering where women inspect not each other's clothes . . . but each other's outlines. A newcomer enters, the eyes of the waiting sorority go straight to the midriff.

You know, you can do some pretty fancy calculating if you know how and what to observe. The beginner, as one might call her, comes blithely in, her hat at a smart angle, picks up one of those mangled periodicals, chooses either the sofa or an armchair, and relaxes into its depths. When her turn is called, she leaps nimbly to her feet, drops the periodical, picks it up with easy agility and skips in through the inner door. The more advanced . . . both in regard to condition and shape . . . say the 5 to 6 monthers, enter in slower motion. That same chic hat has gone further back on the head. She picks up a periodical (undoubtedly the same one as before) chooses a more upright chair, sits with less abandon and when her turn is called, rises slowly, drops the periodical, stoops to pick it up, but finding she can't reach it, bends her knees and retracts it, and with injured dignity plods through the inner door. Last scene of all that ends this strange, eventful history is Mother Nature-Ceres who waddles in, her hat, this time on the back of her head, as if to balance all that precedes her . . . picks up that same copy of Life, looks about for a place to sit down and finding no possible contour model, perches gingerly on the arm of the armchair, when her turn comes, again drops the magazine, again tries to pick it up forward, sideways, at an angle, even knee-bending, utters a mental "To hell with it!" and waddles majestically through that inner door.

Another aspect of the waiting-room I'd like to mention is the receptionist nurse. She has a cozy way of talking shop with the more loquacious clients . . . and she does so in a jargon that seems peculiar to the race of obstetrical nurses. "Mrs. Brown delivered last night," she'll tell someone brightly, or "We're expecting Mrs. White to deliver before tomorrow" . . . (that mail-carrier phraseology . . . "Neither rain nor heat," etc.). Then she uses another interesting term . . . she'll say "We've been having a run on girls lately" or "Better hurry, Mrs. Robinson, we're in the midst of a run on boys!" However, she is always a pleasant and sympathetic person . . . always most co-operative, especially when it comes to that sporadic little drama that is enacted at the beginning of these visits . . . when a patient comes in and, with arch discretion the receptionist asks "Mrs. Jones, have you something for me?" Sometimes a crisis arises when Mrs. Jones, in sudden panic, realizes she hasn't . . . but someone else may have . . . in which event, there is a whispered consultation between Mrs. Jones and the receptionist which ends in the receptionist picking up the phone, dialing a number and an ensuing conversation which may go somewhat like this . . . "Hello? Schrafft's restaurant? I'm calling for Mrs. Cadwallader Jones. She was there for lunch today and she thinks she may have left a small parcel . . . second table to the left."

Of course, conditions may have changed. It was 23 years ago that I began these exhaustive researches . . .

or rather that they were begun on me. When I was in what is laughingly known as the state of expectant motherhood, I was also in the state of having to fulfill the obligations of a theatrical tour. (The actress' greatest difficulty is the acquiring of proper timing. Dramatic critics manage these things better. John Mason Brown's second son, he tells me, was born between *Charley's Aunt* and *George Washington Slept Here*.) For five months, I and Little Nemo toured the Middle-West trailing clouds of sweetness, light and nausea. Being neither a pioneer woman nor a Mme. Schumann-Heink, for whom it was apparently nothing to be a Rhine maiden one evening and the next morning the mother of a new little Heink, I don't recommend a lyceum tour as the best of regimens.

All nonsense aside, I can't tell you how happy and proud I am that you should have chosen me to speak to you this evening. Surely yours must be the most rewarding of all the branches of medicine . . . the happiness you bring us, the health and new life you restore to us. As self appointed spokesman . . . spokeswoman . . . for my sisterhood, may I tell you of our gratitude and affection . . . I'll even say our love . . . (you know it is true that every new mother falls in love for a time with her obstetrician). May I herewith propose a toast from the ladies of America in words which are singularly apt . . . gentlemen of the profession, BOTTOMS UP!!!